THE AUTHORISED VERSION:

❖

A Wonderful and Unfinished History

C. P. HALLIHAN

Trinitarian Bible Society
London, England

The Authorised Version: *A Wonderful and Unfinished History*

A124

ISBN 978-1-86228-049-6

© 2010

Trinitarian Bible Society

Tyndale House, Dorset Road,
London, SW19 3NN, UK

10M/03/11

CONTENTS

TIMELINE

c. 405

Jerome's Latin Vulgate translation of the Bible is produced and in wide circulation.

500

Portions of the Scriptures in five hundred languages available by this time.

1066

William the Conqueror invades England.

1388

Wycliffe's first translation of the entire Bible into English, based on the Latin Vulgate, is published.

1453

Gutenberg invents the printing press. The first book printed is the Bible in Latin—the Gutenberg Bible.

1477-1487

First printed Hebrew Scripture portions.

1483

The Golden Legend, Jacobus de Voragine's 'life of the saints', compiled in the mid-13th century, is printed in English by 'Wyllyam Caxton'. It contains a literal translation of a large portion of the Bible, all of the Pentateuch, and much of the Gospels. At Genesis 3.7 'breeches' is used, to reappear seventy-five years later in the Geneva 'Breeches' Bible.

1509

Accession of King Henry VIII.

1516

Desiderius Erasmus' (1466–1536) first Greek New Testament is printed and published by Froben in Basel; said to have had greater influence on Tyndale than either the Vulgate or Luther.

1517

First Biblia Rabbinica Hebrew Old Testament, printed by Daniel Bomberg, includes the Targums and other traditional explanations.

1518

First separate printed Greek Bible (Septuagint and Koiné New Testament), in Venice by Aldus.

1522

First German (Luther) New Testament, Wittenberg.

1525

William Tyndale's New Testament, based on Erasmus' Greek, completed. His wording and sentence structures are found in most subsequent English translations.

Second Biblia Rabbinica, the first with the Hebrew Masoretic notes, edited by Jacob ben Chayyim.

1530

Tyndale produces his first translation from Hebrew into English when he publishes the Pentateuch.

1535

Myles Coverdale, student of Tyndale, produces a Bible. It includes the Apocrypha.

1536

Tyndale is executed. Tyndale did not live to complete his Old Testament translation, but left manuscripts containing the translation of the historical books from Joshua to 2 Chronicles.

1537

Matthew's Bible printed—Tyndale's translation supplemented by Coverdale's.

1538

Coverdale's Diglot (Latin/English) New Testament.

1539

The Great Bible, basically Matthew's Bible, authorised for public use.

1546

Robert Stephens' first Greek New Testament.
Council of Trent declares Latin Vulgate to be the official version of the Bible in the Roman Catholic Church.

1547

Accession of King Edward VI.

1550

Robert Stephens' third Greek New Testament, considered his most important.

1553

Accession of Queen Mary I.

1557

Geneva New Testament is published by William Whittingham in Geneva, Switzerland. First in English to use verses, and italics for supplied words.

1558

Accession of Queen Elizabeth I.

1560

The Geneva Bible is printed, compiled by exiles from England in Geneva: a meticulous rendering from Greek and Hebrew, set in roman type; one hundred and forty editions are published between 1560 and 1644.

1565

First Beza Greek New Testament.

1568

Bishops' Bible, also called Parker Bible; twenty-two editions are published, the last in 1606; it is not popular, and not well edited.

1584

Plantin's Biblia Hebraica.

1587

First Greek New Testament printed in England.

1598

Beza's last major Greek New Testament. The Authorised Version agrees substantially with this edition.

1603

Accession of King James I of England.

1604

Hampton Court Conference, during which the decision to translate the Bible now known as the Authorised Version was made.

1609–1610

Rheims-Douai Bible is the first complete English Roman Catholic Bible. It is called Rheims-Douai because the New Testament was completed in Rheims, France, in 1582 followed by the Old Testament in Douai, 1609. The fourteen books of the Apocrypha are integrated into the canon of Scripture in the order written rather than kept in a separate section.

1611
AUTHORISED VERSION:

The sixty-six books of Scripture, with the additional fourteen books of the Apocrypha as a separate section (the Apocrypha was only officially removed from the AV in 1885).

1624

Elzevirs' first Greek New Testament.

1629

First Cambridge edition of the AV, revised to correct errors found in earlier editions, particularly in italics and punctuation.

1631

The 'Wicked Bible' printed in London by 'Robert Barker and assigns of John Bill', 8vo;[1] the word 'not' was omitted from the Seventh Commandment; the mistake was discovered before the printing was finished, and copies exist with and without the mistake.

1633

Elzevirs' second Greek New Testament; contains the phrase 'Textus Receptus'.

1637

The 'Religious Bible', so named because of the reading in Jeremiah 4.17 'Because she hath been religious [for 'rebellious'] against me, saith the LORD'. Edinburgh, 8vo.

1638

Cambridge folio edition of the AV, by Thomas Buck and Roger Daniel, clear but smaller roman type, hand-ruled with red lines; text as revised by Dr. Goad, Dr. Ward, Mr. Boise, and Mr. Mead, '…probably the best edition of King James' Version ever published'.[2]

1642

Folio edition of AV published in Amsterdam, first of many editions (Canne's Bibles) originating there, with notes and/or a prologue written by John Canne, prominent among the Brownists.[3]

1643

Soldier's (Cromwell) Pocket Bible (Geneva version).

1655-1657

Walton's London Polyglot.

1717

J. Baskett Imperial Folio ('Vinegar') Bible, two volumes. The Luke 20 chapter heading has 'vinegar' for 'vineyard'—'The Parable of the Vinegar'. It was said to be the most sumptuous of all the Bibles printed at Oxford, and very beautiful. Careless proofreading led to the edition being called 'a Baskett-ful of printers' errors'.

1762

University of Cambridge edition of the AV, edited by Dr. Paris, published in folio and quarto editions; all but six copies of the folio edition were reportedly destroyed by fire.

1763

John Baskerville's Cambridge Bible, a masterpiece of craftsmanship; 1,250 copies were produced, with 500 of them 'remaindered' five years later.

1769

Oxford University edition of the Dr. Paris AV, edited by Dr. Blayney; commonly regarded as the standard edition, from which modern Bibles are printed.

1782

Robert Aitken's Bible, the first English language Bible printed in America (AV without Apocrypha).

1801

The 'Idle Shepherd Bible', so called because of the reading in Zechariah 11.17 'Woe to the idle [for 'idol'] shepherd that leaveth the flock'.

1805

First printing of the New Testament at Cambridge by the newly perfected stereotype process from stereotype plates.

1806

The 'Discharge Bible': 'I discharge [for 'charge'] *thee* before God' in 1 Timothy 5.21.

The 'Standing Fishes Bible': 'and it shall come to pass that the fishes [for 'fishers'] shall stand upon it...' in Ezekiel 47.10. Bible in quarto by the King's Printer, London, reprinted in a quarto edition of 1813, and an octavo edition of 1823.

1807

The 'Ears To Ear Bible': 'Who hath ears to ear [for 'hear'], let him hear' Matthew 13.43. Found in an octavo Bible published by the Oxford Press. The same book contains a more serious blunder in Hebrews 9.14: 'How much more shall the blood of Christ, who through the Eternal Spirit offered himself without spot to God, purge your conscience from good [for 'dead'] works to serve the living God?'.

1831

Bagster's London Polyglot.

1833

AV published at Oxford, an exact reprint, page for page, of the first issue of 1611. Large quarto, with the spelling, punctuation, italics, capitals, and distribution into lines and pages followed with the most scrupulous care; the type is roman not black letter.[4]

1841

English Hexapla New Testament: textual comparison showing Greek and six English translations in parallel columns.

ENDNOTES:

1. The terms folio, quarto (4to) and octavo (8vo) refer to the sizes of books, folio being the largest, followed by quarto and octavo.

2. J. R. Dore, *Old Bibles*, 2nd ed. (London: Basil Pickering, 1888), p. 345.

3. Brownists were nonconformists in the 16th and 17th centuries who separated from the Church of England and formed independent churches in England and Holland.

4. See a discussion of black letter in Appendix 2.

THE AUTHORISED VERSION:

A Wonderful and Unfinished History

Chapter 1
General Introduction

The mighty God, *even* the LORD, hath spoken,
and called the earth from the rising of the sun
unto the going down thereof.

Psalm 50.1

t is the touchstone of Protestant preaching, teaching, life and practice that God has spoken, and that the Bible is the inspired and authoritative record of this. The Bible is 'the holy scriptures, which are able to make thee wise unto salvation through faith which is in Christ Jesus. All scripture *is* given by inspiration of God, and *is* profitable for doctrine, for reproof, for correction, for instruction in righteousness' (2 Timothy 3.15,16). In English we have the inestimable blessing of the Scriptures in our own tongue; in our English Authorised Version, first published in 1611, we have rich, dependable, proven provision, in both text and translation, of the Word of God. It is the crown of one hundred years of labour, from the translating of Tyndale and Coverdale in the early decades of the 16th century to the proofing and polishing by Miles Smith of the Hampton Court committees' work, 1609–1610.

The Reformation deliverance of the Gospel from the lifeless encrustations of medieval Romanism went hand-in-hand with the deliverance of the Scriptures from being a hidden book to being a book for both preacher and people. Recovery of the Gospel as the good news for sinners rather than an instrument of fear and oppression was inseparable from the recovery of the Bible for pulpit, pew, and personal religion. John Wycliffe had laid down markers two hundred years earlier with a clear view of the Scriptures as Christ's Law and commitment to their inherent authority rather than that of the church. He had a very rugged perception of the free Bible as mighty under the hand of God to the pulling down of the strongholds of error and had a burden for their availability in the language of the people. These deep convictions were plainly maintained by God and pursued from Tyndale, Coverdale, Cranmer, Reynolds, and onward.

The Book which brings to us the wonderful works of God has good news to tell, and the history of this Book in our own language is a living part of any worthwhile 'church history'. A sense of history is a great asset to the Christian life because our religion is necessarily historic, God at work in His creation, amongst His creatures, rooted in time and place—real people and events in a way that cannot be said of any other religion. Such a history also brings to view the issues at stake in the proper transmission of the divine record: which texts, translated under which principles, and does it matter?

The principles and procedures for establishing a reliable starting place—a 'ground text'—were not major issues in the beginning of English Bible translation. As is too often the case, it took controversy, opposition and hostility to bring about the realisation that in the English tongue from 1524 to 1604, in Greek textual scholarship from Erasmus 1516 to Beza 1598 and Hebrew manuscript availability from Bomberg in 1517 to Plantin 1584 and on, a settling of the text of Scripture was being accomplished. If 'the mighty God, *even* the LORD, hath spoken', then it is needful to have the record of that speaking not only in our own tongue accurately and faithfully rendered, but also, to all human endeavour, settled in our own tongue.

THE MANUSCRIPTS: HANDWRITTEN SCRIPTURES

With mine own hand

Paul's letter to the Galatians is probably one of the earlier pieces of New Testament writing. In chapter 6, verse 11 he declares 'Ye see how large a letter I have written unto you with mine own hand'.[1] This reminds us of a basic fact to do with the unfolding history of the New Testament, a point so obvious that we easily overlook it. Since printing did not come into being until the mid-15th century, for the first three-quarters of the New Testament's existence it was only available in copies made by hand, truly 'manu-scripts', two Latin words meaning handwritten.[2]

Palestine in Apostolic times was under Roman rule, but for about three hundred years before that it had been under the cultural dominion of Greece. Greek was the everyday language throughout the whole Mediterranean region, acceptable even in Rome. This was the language of 'the fulness of the time', and was the instrument used, under the sovereign Spirit of God, for that written record which is the New Testament of our Lord and Saviour Jesus Christ. Very quickly the burden of copying and translating these Scriptures was taken up by the churches. The practicalities of multiplying and disseminating accurately the written Word of God start us on the path to the present printed editions of our English Authorised Version.

Rolls and papyrus

In New Testament times the Greeks and Romans used papyrus rolls for writing of all sorts. Papyrus is the fibrous pith of a water plant once plentiful in the Nile but scarcely found there now. Two layers of fibres laid at right angles to each other, soaked, squeezed and glued, formed sheets of a material that could receive marks. The side with horizontal fibres was intended for writing (the 'recto') but it was quite possible to use the reverse (the 'verso') as well.

The best quality sheets were those using the largest fibres, and such sheets were joined side-by-side to make rolls of necessary length for the particular document. The longest known roll is 133 feet (40.5m), but the average length of Greek literary rolls was 35 feet (10m). Height was variable, the usual being 10 inches (254mm) although 19 inches (483mm) was not unknown, and there were 'pocket' scrolls of only 5 inches (127mm). On such papyrus rolls the writing was most often in columns 2.5 to 3 inches (64 to 76mm) wide.

There were margins between columns and at the top and bottom for annotations and the insertion of corrections. Ordinarily, rolls were written only on one side, but if material was scarce or there was a lot to be said, they could be written 'within and without' (Ezekiel 2.10) or 'within and on the backside' (Revelation 5.1). Sometimes the verso of an existing work was used for more writing—one early 4th-century manuscript of Hebrews is on the back of a 3rd-century condensed Livy.[3]

Taking average figures as a guide we can visualise the autographs of the New Testament (that is, the first written documents made by John, Luke, etc.) written in this manner. An epistle such as 2 Thessalonians would be contained on a 5-foot roll of five columns only. Romans would need 11.5 feet, Revelation 15 feet, Mark 19 feet, and Luke 32 feet! So long as the papyrus roll was the medium of literature, the various copies of the books of the New Testament almost certainly circulated separately, and each book has its own 'history'. Indeed, until the use of the printing press in the 15th century, few Christian communities and even fewer individuals possessed all the canonical books.

Imagine the difficulties of using scrolls. I can mention

Papyrus reed beds along the Nile (below) and a detailed sample of papyrus paper showing the pattern of fibres (right)

Revelation 5.1 or Ezekiel 2.10 and expect you easily to find this reference in a Bible. But what if you had a collection of scrolls to sort through to find the right book, and rather than pages to turn had to roll the scroll out to where you think the particular passage might be! Remember, there are no 'reader aids' or 'editorial input'—and

> Noseparationofwordspunctuationminimallatercorrectionsattopandbot tomscarcelyanycapitalsorindicationofparagraphsandnochapteror versenumbersandthelinesdontalwaysrunthesameway.[4]

How difficult to find the exact verse—perhaps we should excuse those early Christian writers who quote rather 'freely' or sometimes quote the same verse slightly differently, and often just say the quotation is found 'somewhere in Luke'.

Codices and vellum

Christians were particularly concerned to improve on this situation. As early as the 2nd century AD 'codex' experiments were tried. A papyrus codex is made up of sheets of papyrus folded once into a 'quire' or gathering, like a gigantic scrapbook; this is in fact the basis of the book as we have it today. For this we have the church to thank: it was the desire of the churches for 'user friendly' and portable Scriptures that helped establish this now universal system of book construction. Truly, in the providence of our mighty God, the full record of His Word deserves, even in this small but significant point, to be called 'The Book'.

Quires were fastened by threads through the inner margin, like a modern stapling process, and sometimes monstrous fifty-sheet folds were used in a single cumbersome quire. One famous papyrus codex referred to as P46 in the cataloguing system for these documents, and called Chester Beatty II, was once a single quire codex of one hundred and four leaves—only eighty-six are known to exist now. A more usual format was quires of eight to twelve leaves, joined as needed.

The main advantage of this was that more material could be contained, and more easily consulted, without the volume becoming unmanageable. P46, referred to above, originally contained all the Pauline epistles except Timothy and Titus. As a scroll this would have been some 60 feet in length—or at least two 30 footers. The five separate scrolls needed for early copies of the Gospels and Acts were replaced in the 3rd century by one codex, P45 (Chester Beatty I).

Another step in the external form of New Testament material came with the 'official' establishment of Christianity under the reign of Emperor Constantine, in the 4th century. The status of the Christian documents changed abruptly, and the wholesale destruction of books that had accompanied earlier persecutions ceased (for a while). Demand began to grow, instead, throughout the empire as Christianity became respectable.

Just at this point the book makers reintroduced vellum as the writing material. It had been in use for some time, in Pergamum from about 190 BC (and it is a form of the name of that town which gives us the name 'parchment' for vellum), but never on a large scale. Vellum is made from the skins of cattle, sheep and goats, especially young ones. The hair is scraped off, the skins washed, rubbed with pumice, and dressed with chalk, giving an almost white sheet, durable and easy to write on in black or certain other colours. Once Christianity became an imperial religion, the physical appearance of the books took on an importance that had not been there before, and some of the vellum codices of Scripture are extremely beautiful things to look at, though not necessarily reliable or accurate because of that!

Just to complete the picture, note that 'paper', a Chinese cloth-based refinement of the papyrus writing material, appeared in the West in the 12th century, but from the 4th to 15th centuries vellum was the preferred material.

Part of P46 showing 2 Corinthians 11.33-12.9

Hebrew too

The hand copying of the Hebrew Scriptures was always a more circumspect work. There was never the urgent pressure to multiply and disseminate as came with the New Testament. Every man was to make or have made a copy of the Torah (Law) for his personal use (Deuteronomy 31.19[5]), a work that would be meticulous and unhurried. Scroll copies for Temple, king (Deuteronomy 17.18–19), and, later, synagogues and scribes, were made with reverential, word-and-consonant-counting care from a preserved exemplar[6] (Deuteronomy 31.26). It is a fascinating story in its own right, but for now I record only that the Hebrew Scriptures, which we know as our Old Testament, continued to be copied into the Christian era.

After the destruction of the Temple in AD 70 the Jews were exceedingly anxious to maintain their correct text. From about AD 90 the addition of 'points' to show vowel sounds and various stress and cadence indicators was introduced into the consonantal Hebrew to ensure the correct understanding of the text. Careful copying continued, and the Hebrew Scriptures were certainly known to the Christian world. Origen included a Hebrew text in his six-column *Hexapla* around AD 240, and Jerome used Hebrew directly (rather than the early Greek

translation of the Old Testament, the Septuagint) as a source for his Bethlehem Latin Bible of AD 405. After that it became more difficult to acquire either the language or copies of the Hebrew text in a Christian setting; even the attempt would attract suspicion and hostility from Jew and Christian alike. But the time would come.

Destruction of the Temple, AD 70

Translations

Scripture, existing in three languages and offering translations within itself (e.g., Matthew 1.23; Mark 5.41, 15.22,34; John 1.38,41,42, 9.7; Acts 4.36, 9.36, 13.8), is inherently translatable, and response to the need for Scriptures in the vernacular (or common language of a people) is as old as the New Testament.[7] Early translation of the New Testament from Greek into Latin began about AD 180, not in Italy, but in North Africa. Such translation of the Old and New Testaments into Latin is referred to as the 'Old Latin'; both Testaments were in fact translated from Greek sources. Around 300 there was a translation of the New Testament into Syriac, the 'Old Syriac', called also the Peshitta—that is, the 'simple' version.[8] There were also four versions in Coptic, the language spoken in four dialects in Egypt, and other early translations in Armenian, Georgian, Ethiopic, Slavonic and Gothic.

The most significant and influential work began in 380, when Jerome was translating anew into Latin the Old Testament from Hebrew and the New Testament from Greek. This return to Hebrew rather than the standard Greek Septuagint as the proper source for Old Testament translation, although beyond doubt the correct procedure, was strongly resisted and resented at the time. There were several Latin editions, and this version, styled the 'Vulgate' because it was the vulgar or commonly used language, became the Bible of Western Christianity until the Protestant Reformation in the 1500s.[9]

Jerome at work on the Vulgate

Apart from the long, slow adulteration of the Vulgate text over the next thousand years,[10] the venerated Latin text generated problems for translation all through that time. From Augustine to Erasmus, Bible translation never escaped the incubus of Latin as the source text. Thus, increasingly slanted

interpretations in the Vulgate made their way into the few non-Latin translations that were produced.

This historical period of scholarship, in very general terms, is that of the Byzantine Empire, centred in Byzantium, formerly Constantinople. Most Greek scholarship was focused there; and literature, including many Biblical texts, were never carried beyond the area, and thus, for a time, were beyond easy reach of the Western world.

Early English endeavours

First the apologies. Without intent to offend, the word 'English' is being used as a catch-all for indigenous languages spoken in Britain and 'adjacent islands' in these early times. Please forgive the chronologically inexact use of 'English' to include many lands, languages, scripts and dialects such as Celtic, Cymric, shades of Saxon, Irish, Welsh: it is done to save continual distinctions having to be drawn, rather than through ignorance or indifference.

There were, then, yearnings and strivings toward the provision of English language Scriptures quite early in the Gospel history of the land. Chrysostom (347–407) hints of English Scriptures in Britain almost as soon as the Gospel arrived, and Gildas (504–570) certainly speaks in his *Ruin of Britain* of Scriptures and pastors being butchered together in British towns during the Diocletian persecution (284–305).[11]

The goal of vernacular Scriptures was pursued throughout the so-called Dark Ages, the ubiquitous but unhelpful title used vaguely to cover the thousand years from the decline of Rome in the 5th century to the fall of Constantinople in 1453. Certainly there are distressingly dark aspects of the history of that time, but the maintenance of Greek learning in Byzantium, the eager incorporation of Indian learning into Muslim scholarship, and, perhaps more significant for our immediate purposes, the rugged sanctity, scholarship, mission and manuscript work of Celtic Ireland must not be ignored or minimised.

Roman legions left Britain in 409–410, to guard Italy after Alaric I of the Visigoths (370–410) captured and sacked Rome. The Roman garrison forces in Britain had long fluctuated between thirty and fifty thousand men, drawn from all over the Empire, with the attendant family, administrative and trading communities—and the ongoing settlement of time-expired legionaries. There is plain evidence that amongst these numbers there were Christians. Alban[12] was of the noble army of martyrs.

It is also interesting that Constantine, who was Emperor from 306 to 337 and legitimised Christianity throughout the Roman Empire, was first declared Emperor by legionary forces at York. British 'bishops' had been present at the Council of Arles, in 314.[13] One

Constantine AD 272-337

hundred years later Augustine wrote his *City of God* in the aftermath of the destruction of Rome, and our nation provided a theological antagonist for him: Pelagius[14] was from Britain; he taught in Rome and died in 418, Augustine in 430.

Archaeology in southern Britain has revealed traces of buildings dedicated to Christian use, but equally, if not more significantly, rooms set aside in homes for Christian meeting: small chapels and house meetings are no new thing. These brethren would mostly be content with the Latin Scriptures, maybe even the Jerome Vulgate, hot from Bethlehem.

Amongst those left in Britain after 410 there were many Celts, and a 'Romano-British' residual culture lingered on to face the increasing incursions of Jutes, Angles and Saxons. Within that culture Christianity continued, refreshed and renewed from time to time by Irish missions. This Irish connection is the genesis of some of the earliest English fragments of Scripture, from interlinear[15] editions to magnificent illuminated[16] manuscripts.

There was, then, a growing incentive for, at least, paraphrasing Scripture into the English languages of that time. In the struggle to produce the Scriptures, the Psalms and the Gospels have long been favoured as the first necessities for truth and devotion, and so it was here. In the 7th century the monk Caedmon made a metrical version of some portions of Scripture, and Theodore of Tarsus (d. 690), seventh Archbishop of Canterbury, urged upon all parents the need to teach their children the Lord's Prayer in the common tongue. Bede translated the Gospels into English, supposedly finishing the Gospel according to John on his deathbed in 735. The chronicler William of Malmesbury, 1090–1143, assures us that King Alfred, 849–899, had memorised the New Testament, Psalms and other Old Testament portions. Having rendered the Ten Commandments into English, Alfred was engaged at the time of his death in a new translation of the Psalms.

Title page for the Gospel according to Matthew, Lindisfarne Gospels

Some interlinear translations have survived from the 10th century, the Lindisfarne Gospels produced by Aldred (*c.* 950) being the most famous. Aelfric (*c.* 955–1020) made rough and idiomatic translations of Scripture portions, two of which have survived until today. Almost three hundred years later, William of Shoreham and Richard Rolle each translated the Psalter. Rolle's work included a verse-by-verse commentary, and both these Psalters were still popular at the time of John Wycliffe.

Copying the Scriptures

It must be acknowledged that the language used was quite variable throughout the 'kingdoms' in Britain. An 'English' document produced in Wessex would not necessarily be useful in Mercia or Strathclyde or Northumbria. We would not find any of these older forms easy to the eye, ear or tongue now!

Compare these renderings of Luke 2.7,11:

11th century: Wessex

and heo cende hyre frumcennedan sunu. and hine mid cildclaþum bewand. and hine on binne alede. forþam þe hig næfdon rum on cumena huse…forþam todæg eow ys hælend acenned. se is drihten crist on dauides ceastre

14th century: Wycliffe

& she childide hir first goten sone, & wlappede hym in cloþis & putte hym in a cracche, for þer was not place to hym in þe comun stable…for a saueour is born to day to vs, þat is crist a lord in þe cite of dauid

and for contrast:

16th century: Tyndale

And she brought forth her fyrst begotten sonne and wrapped him in swadlynge cloothes and layed him in a manger because ther was no roume for them within in the ynne…for vnto you is borne this daye in the cite of David a saueoure which is Christ ye lorde.

Tyndale may look quaint, but is quite comprehensible—one can read it aloud and hearers would understand. But without some familiarity with the sounds and orthography of Anglo-Saxon English, it is none too easy to read Wessex or Wycliffe.

An Anglo-Saxon manuscript of 995 renders John 3.16 thus:

God lufode middan-eard swa, dat he seade his an-cennedan sunu, dat nan ne forweorde de on hine gely ac habbe dat ece lif.

And around 1200 Orm brought John 3 to the English of his day:

Thurrh thatt te Laferrd seggde thus	*In that the Lord said thus*
Till Nicodem withth worde	*To Nicodemus with word*
Swa lufede the Laferrd Godd	*So loved the Lord God*
The Werelld tatt he sennde	*The world that he sent*
His aghenn sune Allmahtig Godd	*His own son Almighty God*
To wurrthen mann on erthe	*To become man on earth*
To lesenn mannkinn thurrh hiss death	*To release mankind through his death*
Ut off the defless walde	*Out of the devil's power*
Thatt whase trowwenn shall on himm	*That whosoever shall believe on him*
Wel mughe wurrthenn borrghenn	*Surely may become saved*

ENDNOTES:

1. See also 1 Corinthians 16.21, 2 Thessalonians 3.17 and Philemon 19. It is the seal of his authority.

2. Perhaps it could have been from Greek roots *cheiro-graphs*, meaning just the same thing!

3. Papyrus 13 is a manuscript fragment containing portions of the book of Hebrews. On the back of this fragment are portions of the *Epitome of Livy*, the pre-Christian history of Rome.

4. Compare formal Chinese for a language with no word boundaries.

5. According to Jewish tradition as recorded in the Talmudic *Sanh.* 21b, the 'song' included the Torah (Pentateuch) in its entirety.

6. An exemplar is a manuscript that serves as the standard edition of a document, and which is often used for copying.

7. Is it not ironic that where the Gospel went by word of mouth, the immediate hunger was for the independent stability and endurance of the written word of Scripture, whereas today vast sums are spent trying to make the written word look and sound like a short-lived, ever-shifting spoken form!

8. Syriac 'missionaries' went through Mesopotamia bearing their news to India, probably China too, as well as northwards into Armenia and Georgia.

9. Please see *Quarterly Record* no. 579, April to June 2007, for more information on the Latin Scriptures.

10. The Vulgate of Jerome is scarcely to be recognised in the tired and corrupted Latin Vulgate edition affirmed by the Council of Trent.

11. For additional information, see Paul Halsall's *Internet Medieval Sourcebook* at www.fordham.edu/halsall/Sbook.html and search for 'Scripture'.

12. Alban, who died in the mid to late 3rd or early 4th century AD, is considered Britain's first Christian martyr. He is said to have hidden a Christian fugitive and then taken his place before the courts, incurring the wrath of the magistrate who had Alban beheaded in the fugitive's stead.

13. The Council of Arles in 314 formally declared Donatism, which taught that only the absolutely pure and blameless could be in the true church, and that only sacraments administered by the pure and blameless were valid, to be heresy.

14. Pelagius highlights the land/language confusion very well. He was from Britain—or was he from Breton? In Rome and during his short time in Carthage (almost a pen's throw from Augustine in Hippo) he was called Brittus, but they almost certainly meant Welsh, with 'Pelagius' a strange Latinised form of Morgan. When he got to Palestine to wrangle with Jerome, he was called a foolish Scot—but by that, of course, Jerome really meant Irish.

15. A Biblical interlinear is a copy of the Scriptures containing the Biblical language text with a very literal translation of each word underneath that word.

16. An illuminated manuscript has decorations, often highly ornate and not always Christian, adorning its margins and sometimes forming the first letters of books or chapters.

Chapter 2

John Wycliffe and the English Bible

'I believe that in the end the Truth will conquer.'[1]

hen there were two popes, John Wycliffe said that there was no Scriptural basis for even one. When only a few of the better educated could read the Bible—only available in Latin—John Wycliffe said that everyone should have the Bible in their own language. When challenged over his views, John Wycliffe said that the Scriptures alone were his source and authority. All this was a century before Erasmus, Luther, Tyndale or Calvin were born, and John Wycliffe (1320–1384) is the most conspicuous name in the history of the English Bible up to the Reformation. He was concerned not only for the availability of the Scriptures in the common tongue, but also for the fruit of it in the application of Scripture to every part of life, personal and ecclesiastical.

In course of time, medieval England had come to terms with the Conquest of 1066. The use of French as the polite language continued for a long time, but the writings of William Langland and Geoffrey Chaucer were making English respectable. The Norman royal line had become the House of Anjou—the Plantagenets—and struggles for territory in France rumbled on. In 1215 the English barons gathered at Runnymede and obliged John to sign Magna Carta. This first small step towards redefining royal power said in effect, 'this nation, land and people, isn't yours to give, nor the pope's to take'.

However, the chief enemy of all countries in medieval Europe was always the current pope. Money was siphoned away through strange taxes imposed and collected by the Roman church, helped by the appointment of non-resident foreign clergy to church posts. There was need of someone to say not just that the church was wrong about this or that particular, but simply—this church is wrong. The church was wrong because it was comprehensively, demonstrably, un-Biblical—in fact no church at all. There was need for God, who commanded the light to shine out of darkness, to give again by the mirror of His Word 'the light of the knowledge of the glory of God in the face of Jesus Christ' (2 Corinthians 4.6).

John Wycliffe (1320–1384)

John Wycliffe (1320–1384)[2]

When Wycliffe was at Oxford University, it was the time of Thomas Bradwardine (1290–1349). Bradwardine insisted that God's grace is the ultimate necessity and cause in salvation, a truth which found a ready place in the thinking of the young Wycliffe. He also embraced Bradwardine's insistence that dependence upon outward forms should not be confused with true religion of the heart.

Wycliffe loved the Scriptures, and in his growing practice of reading the Bible in public, and growing confidence in referring to the Scriptures as the sole authority, he earned the name 'Gospel Doctor'. His determination that the truth of the Scripture should be widely and soundly preached, as well as read, grew. Both the learned and the common people heard him gladly as he settled confidently on the Bible and its authority. He denounced the ecclesiastical world for effectively banishing the Scriptures, and for making the church of Christ a world power.

Hostility was inevitable, and in 1377 Wycliffe, rector of Lutterworth in Leicestershire, was summoned to appear at St. Paul's, London, to answer charges against his teachings. He was dismissed with warnings, and went about his business, which brought the papal authorities to demand that the bishops, university and king should apprehend John Wycliffe on the pope's behalf.

Archbishop Sudbury summoned Wycliffe again to appear, this time at Lambeth in 1378. There, one hundred and fifty years in anticipation of Luther's justly famed confession ('Here I stand—I can do no other'), John Wycliffe declared that he followed only the Scriptures, and if shown to be wrong by the Scriptures he would retract his teachings. Scripture alone was the fountain of truth and foundation of authority, and anything not agreeable to Scripture should neither be imposed nor obeyed, in things temporal or in things spiritual. Supported by Joan of Kent, the widow of Edward, the Black Prince, Wycliffe received another formal admonition but was released.

St Mary's, Lutterworth

Preaching, teaching, writing and translation work would occupy Wycliffe, living at Lutterworth, for the last years of his life. Addressing the leading issues—the papacy, the mass, and the monks: their corruptions and their lack of Biblical foundation—Wycliffe laid the axe to the root of the tree. He was learning and teaching the magnificent truth that the visible church, in all its parts, powers and persons, is ever subject to evaluation and reformation in the light of Scripture only.

The truth of Scripture and the Lollard[3] Bible

The mainspring of Wycliffe's mature work was that the Scriptures are the foundation of all doctrine. His 1378 work *De veritate Sacrae Scripturae* (*On the Truth of Sacred Scripture*) describes the Bible as being directly from God Himself, timeless, unchanging, free from error and contradictions, containing only truth, accepting no addition, suffering no subtraction. All must be taken equally, absolutely, without qualification. Scripture is the law of Christ, the truth, and must be placed above all human writings. Without knowledge of the Bible there can be no peace, no real and abiding good; it contains all that is necessary for the salvation of men. It alone is infallible, and therefore is the one authority for the faith. Just as a true Christian will be one who finds his faith in the light of Scripture, so a true shepherd of Christians will be one who feeds his flock on the Word of God.

Wycliffe's next step was inevitable, and utterly at odds with medieval Romanist views. The Bible must be available for the people in their mother tongue. Wycliffe did not want to circulate careful Latin selections to an elite, educated few. He was of the same mind as Tyndale later, that the Scriptures should be widely available. Even ploughboys should know the truth of the Gospel and the errors of their supposed guides.

A page from a Wycliffe Bible showing the beginning of the Gospel according to Mark

The first Wycliffe Bible, *c.* 1388, comprises a revision of Wycliffe's translation of the New Testament (*c.* 1382), together with one of the Old Testament done by a friend, Nicholas of Hereford. This Old Testament is sometimes held up to ridicule because of a too rigid following of the word order of the Latin Bible, making it clumsy and awkward reading in English. But Wycliffe's New Testament is more boldly and readably English, though still carrying the problems of having been translated from Latin. The work was soon revised and it is the later, smoother, version which is the 'Lollard Bible', widely diffused through the 15th century. As every copy was handwritten it was never a 'mass-produced' book.

Opposition was fierce and merciless. Possession of such a Bible, let alone reading it or revealing a sympathy with its teaching, was potentially a matter of death, and many died. There was a very dark side to this work, as men in terror for their lives recanted, some becoming accusers, denouncers and persecutors of their former Lollard companions and Wycliffe's teachings. Nevertheless, in England now the sure Word was heard in a familiar tongue: men began to give heed as to a light that shineth in a dark place.[4]

Lollard preachers

John Wycliffe in Lutterworth gave himself to the care of souls, toiling as preacher and teacher to the people. He wished to be done with the existing church hierarchy, for it had no warrant in Scripture. Instead he would put in its place the 'poor priests' who lived in poverty, and preached the Gospel. These itinerant preachers published abroad among the people the teachings of Wycliffe, even 'Christe's lore' (law). They went two-by-two, barefoot, wearing long red robes, and carrying a staff in symbolic reference to their shepherd calling. Passing from place to place with the Bible, they preached Christ's law, and the Scripture as the all-sufficient source of it. They suffered and they were killed.

These dear souls carried the torch of the English Bible from the 14th to the 16th centuries, and when the printing presses began to serve the Protestant Reformation, they handed that torch on to Tyndale, Coverdale, the Geneva scholars, and so on. All of the later workers were reaping where they had sown. Wycliffe, his Bible, his 'poor priests' and the Lollards spread tinder through the land,

Wycliffe sending out the Lollards

and into Europe through John Hus. It was well dried by the heat of persecution. Then, after a brief 'night watch' of one hundred years, the Lord was pleased to kindle that which He had so long prepared, and the Reformation was begun.

On the last Lord's Day of December 1384 Wycliffe was stricken with a paralysis whilst conducting the service of the Lord's Supper in Lutterworth Church. Carried by his friends to his own bed, he died peacefully there on December 31st. The church powers forbad, yet again, the translation, making, reading or possession of an English Bible. A papal council of 1415, the one which deceitfully lured John Hus to a martyr's death,[5] declared Wycliffe a heretic, and demanded that his remains be exhumed and destroyed. In 1428 this was done, and Wycliffe's bones were burnt, with the ashes cast into the River Swift at Lutterworth.

Summary

B. F. Westcott wrote in 1868, 'The History of the English Bible begins with the work of Tindale, and not with that of Wycliffe'.[6] This dismissal is peremptorily fierce. In the history of the transmission of an English text, such a 'sidelining' may be acceptable, but in context of a massive contribution to the making of a way, a will, under God for an English Bible, it is a draconian levelling. Westcott, along with so many others, seems to have ignored Wycliffe's massive contribution to the doctrine of Scripture, which must always go hand in hand with the text of Scripture.

Wycliffe's mighty labours also serve, however, to underscore the great problem of the accuracy and authenticity of all these older English manuscript versions. They were all derived from the Latin Vulgate, not the Biblical language texts. Not only was the starting point not as accurate as it should have been, a translation of a translation, but the corruptions in and variations between copies of the Vulgate were growing out of hand in the passage of time.[7] There is, at this point in the history of the text of Scripture, great need: for a method of reproduction which will anchor the text in a stable and accurately repeatable form, and for a return to the awareness and use of the Biblical languages as the only authoritative basis for translation.[8]

Overall it is helpful to remember that the influence of Wycliffe, his Bible and the Lollards, continued right through into Tyndale's time: the establishment attitudes, whether ecclesiastical or political, were the same throughout. As in 1429 one Margery Baxter was indicted for inviting her maid to a Bible reading, so in 1514 Richard Hun was imprisoned and done to death as a Lollard. To be 'known' to the believers as a reader of the English Scriptures was to find acceptance; to be so known to the authorities was a great danger. When a fierce proclamation against Tyndale's Testament was delivered in 1529, the destruction of all heresies and errors 'commonly called Lollardies' was equally urged.

In December 1554, in Mary's bloodstained reign, Parliament re-enacted the penal statutes against Lollards, and in February 1555 John Rogers, companion of Tyndale and Coverdale, was burnt at the stake. We see in Wycliffe's life and times the prologue to the Reformation, and note the bitter hostility of 'professionals' and 'experts' to the presentation of the Bible as being the exclusive reference and authority for the 'lore of Christ'.

ENDNOTES:

1. Wycliffe in a 1381 statement to the Duke of Lancaster.

2. *Quarterly Record* no. 565, October to December 2003, has a fuller treatment of Wycliffe.

3. The Lollards, 14th-century followers of John Wycliffe, were early reformers of the church. The name has several possible sources. The most likely is from a Dutch term meaning 'someone who mutters', but it could also be from the Latin referring to a noxious weed, from the Middle English referring to a vagabond or lazy beggar, or from the name of a 14th-century monk who converted to Waldensianism and was burnt at the stake. The term 'Lollard' was generally used for anyone without a respectable academic background (e.g., they could not read Latin), and was later applied to followers of Wycliffe. By the mid-15th century, it included anyone considered to be a heretic by the Roman Catholic Church.

4. Being handwritten and copied, there are several 'versions' of the 14th-century Lollard Bible, early and late copies, in which the basic work of Wycliffe, Purvey and Hereford can be traced in differing proportions. There was no complete edition published in print until 1850, but James Thomas' *A Treatise on the Corruption of Scripture, Councils, and Fathers, by the Prelates, Pastors, and Pillars of the Church of Rome, for Maintenance of Popery and Irreligion* (London: printed for Mathew Lownes, 1612) quotes passages from Wycliffe. The New Testament was published in 1731, 1810 and 1848 in different versions, and it also appeared in Bagster's English Hexapla, 1841. Adam Clarke's commentary uses Wycliffe in the Song of Solomon. When the 'definitive' edition of this Bible was published by Oxford University Press in 1850, the editors, Forshall and Madden, examined one hundred and seventy manuscripts in a twenty-two-year labour.

5. He was burnt as a heretic because of his espousal of Lollard views and his stern hostility to the greedy ambition of priests. His followers soon began to translate the Bible into Czech, and their New Testament was published in 1475.

6. B. F. Westcott, *A General View of the History of the English Bible*, 3rd edn. (London: Macmillan and Co., 1905), p. 316.

7. Please see *Quarterly Record* no. 579, April to June 2007, for further information on Latin Scriptures.

8. An interesting observation, using modern terminology—all translation before Wycliffe reads like poetic paraphrase. Wycliffe, in terms of the text before him (which, of course, was the Latin), approximated more nearly to a formal equivalence approach than these earlier attempts at translation. Unlike his predecessors, Wycliffe had a thoroughgoing doctrine of Scripture driving him to a carefulness that resulted in this more formal equivalence.

Chapter 3
Technology, Scholarship and Martyrdom:

The Printed English Bible

A need supplied: printing

he privilege of viewing the unfolding of all history as the living God at work—dealing with His people and His Word in the midst of a careless, indifferent, hostile world—is a glad source of refreshment and ground of praise for the believer. This is particularly true of the amazing convergence of events affecting the history of the Bible text in the 15th and 16th centuries.

To meet the need outlined in the previous chapter, we see that in Europe conditions were just ready for the large scale production of texts. The requirements for book printing were available. Paper was being produced and used in Europe.[1] Artists had invented an oil-based ink which could be adapted for printing on paper and vellum, instead of the earlier insubstantial watery ink. There were presses in use for printing designs on textiles, adaptable for paper printing, and workers were already making metal plates to use for stamping the covers of manuscript books. The time was ripe for Johann Gutenberg's invention of printing with movable type. Such was the impact of printing and its use for the Bible and religious material generally, that a contemporary verse expressed this admiration of

> *…the presse,*
>
> *The worth whereof no tongue can well expresse*
> *So much it doth, and workes so readily:*
> *For which let's give unto the Lord all praise,*
> *That thus hath bless'd us in these latter daies.*[2]

Gutenberg, born in Mainz around 1397, was trained as a goldsmith. He set up a foundry, with press, in Mainz, and experimented with the concept of printing with movable metal type. Finally, around 1453, he printed the *editio princeps*[3] of the Latin Bible. Problematically for him, he was heavily in debt and in 1455 his creditor and partner, Johann Fust, closed on the loans. Gutenberg did finish

Johann Gutenberg (c.1397-1468)

printing the Bible, but lost his press equipment and metal fonts to Fust. After this he seems to have wandered to other cities, teaching the new technique of printing, and died in his native town in 1468.

The Englishman William Caxton (1422–1491) acquired the technique of letterpress printing when he was in Cologne, 1471–1472. In association with the Flemish calligrapher Colard Mansion, Caxton set up a press in Bruges, printing the first books in English there. Then, in 1476, he set up the press in Westminster and printed the first book in England[4] in 1477. Caxton was very cautious about the political consequences of any attempt to print an English Bible, Lollardy and the Wycliffe Bible being so heavily proscribed. However, in his first edition of the *Golden Legend*, 1483, he embedded large portions of Scripture material (the greater part of the Old Testament in fact) translated into English from the Latin and French sources of Jacobus de Voragine.

Gutenberg Bible

William Caxton

Printed books quickly became an accepted and regular part of life in Europe. Indeed, by 1501 there were a thousand printing shops in Europe, which had produced twenty million copies of thirty-five thousand titles[5]. Bible production in multiple copies of the same text was now possible,[6] but one more piece was needful to put the English Bible on track: the break from the Latin text as the basis of translation.

Another need supplied: the Biblical languages

The year 1453 marked not only the first printing of the Bible, but also the overthrow of the city of Constantinople. This city on the northern shore of the Bosphorus had been Byzantium, which today is Istanbul. For a thousand years Byzantium had maintained an empire, derived from the Roman Empire, nominally Christian, and wholly Greek in language, literature and culture. The burgeoning strength of the Ottoman Muslim Empire under Mehmet II, centred in Anatolia (modern Turkey), laid siege to the waning culture of Byzantium and in fifty-four days the city fell. So huge were the effects of this event that some historians have used it as marking the beginning of 'modern' history.[7]

For the history of the text of Scripture, the significance is that Greek scholars, scholarship and literature surged westward seeking refuge. On the European stage, the scene was set for the flowering of the Renaissance; for the Western churches the original language texts of the New Testament were brought again to mind, with men capable of instructing others in them.[8] Many of these displaced scholars went to Italy, from New Rome (Constantinople) to Old Rome. The first part of the Bible to be printed in Greek was a Greek and Latin Psalter of 1481 in Milan, but work on the printed New Testament was soon in hand.

John Colet, 1467–1519, will serve us well to illustrate events of those times. He was the eldest son of the Lord Mayor of London, Sir Henry Colet, educated at St. Anthony's school and Magdalen College, Oxford, becoming M.A. in 1490. In 1493 he went to Paris and then to Italy—a journey abroad seeking the 'new learning'— and then returning to London, Oxford and Cambridge to spread it, which was a familiar path for England's serious scholars at that time. In Italy he was able to study the rudiments of Greek[9] sufficiently well that he later assisted Thomas Linacre in the production of the first printed Greek grammar in England.

Colet became acquainted with the teaching of Savonarola, and with Erasmus whom Colet strongly influenced and drew to England. John Colet's most significant contribution towards the English Reformation was his reading the Greek New Testament with his students at Oxford in a momentous lecture series on Romans in which he expounded the text in accordance with the plain meaning of the words. Such activity was strictly forbidden by the church, but subsequently Colet went even further, reading the Scriptures, in English, in public, at St Paul's Cathedral.[10] In this open violation of the church's 'Latin-only' policy, Colet demonstrated the hunger for the Gospel in English, fuelling the growing fire of the Reformation.

John Colet 1467–1519

As Greek studies particularly flourished in Italy, so did Hebrew studies in Germany. The shaking of Renaissance society made it just a little easier for Jew and Christian to collaborate in study, but there were also some outstanding Jewish converts to the Gospel. Printing had also brought the full Hebrew text, with vowels and accents, to be published at Soncino, in Lombardy, Italy, at the *Casa degli Stampatori*[11] Printers' House, where the first complete Hebrew Old Testament in the world was printed in 1488. Other editions followed, crowned by the work of Felix Pratensis, a 'Jewish' Christian. This was published by Daniel Bomberg in 1517, and then, edited by Jacob ben Chayyim, in 1525. This later edition became the 'received text' of the Hebrew Old Testament.

Across the turn of the century, from about 1480 to 1530, there was a growing supply of grammars and lexicons in both the Biblical languages, as well as early printings of the text. Now we have the appointed conjunction: the renewal of Greek and Hebrew learning and printing, and the availability of printed Greek and Hebrew Testaments. There was also the Christian scholars' fast-growing need to translate anew from a clear ground-text.

Furthermore, the appetite for Scriptures in the common tongues of Europe was growing wherever opportunity allowed. Erasmus of Rotterdam and Ximenes of Complutum (Alcala) in Spain, were working towards the printed text[12] of the New Testament in the dawning years of the 16th century. Ximenes completed his *Polyglot*, which included a Greek New Testament, a year before Erasmus printed his Greek; but Ximenes did not publish, so the first actually published Greek New Testament was that of Erasmus in 1516.

None of these three men—Colet, Erasmus or Ximenes—ever made the complete, needful break with Rome, and yet in the sovereign providence of God they gave the chief provision to complete the Reformation task: the Greek New Testament. The English Reformers received their work gladly, the better to learn of Christ and the better to preach the Gospel, becoming mighty through God to the pulling down of strongholds (2 Corinthians 10.4). So that the Gospel might not perish with them, the Reformers used this Greek New Testament as the sound basis of the New Testament in English, translated and printed for the use of preachers, ploughboys and kings.

The men supplied

1. TYNDALE

William Tyndale was born in Gloucestershire about 1484 or 1494; North Nibley, between Wotton-under-Edge and Dursley on the edge of the Cotswolds, has a major claim to be his birthplace. He seems to have entered on studies at Oxford at a very early age, excelling in them. Colet's earlier influence in Oxford had produced much sympathy for the 'new teachings' amongst the students, and much suspicion amongst the authorities. This perhaps accounts for Tyndale's move to Cambridge, where he found the strong influence of Erasmus' teachings and the companionship of such figures as Bilney, Latimer, Frith, Coverdale and Ridley. These were the first fruits of the 'purer faith' of the English Reformation, openly and avowedly in Christ through faith alone, and, increasingly openly, out of Rome.

From Erasmus and Colet the need was realised for a clear Scripture source in the Biblical languages. From their own preaching and readings they all saw that, as Tyndale later wrote in his preface to the Pentateuch, '...it was impossible to establish the lay people in any truth, except the Scripture were plainly laid before their eyes in their mother tongue...'

After university Tyndale was chaplain and tutor to a family in Little Sodbury, near Bristol. The

William Tyndale

family was sympathetic to his teachings, but too many visitors were not, and Tyndale formed the conviction he must translate the New Testament into English, to be a light in a dark place, to convince the gainsayers!

Seeking help from the Bishop of London, Cuthbert Tunstall, in 1523, proved a fruitless journey, but further fellowship with Frith and others confirmed his burden. If it could not be done in England, it would be done elsewhere. He went to Hamburg in 1524, visited Luther in Wittenberg, and began to print an English Testament in Cologne, 1525. Intrigue forced him to flee to Worms, and there two editions of the English Testament were printed; by 1526 there was a covert colportage line smuggling them into England.

Tyndale's scholarship is beyond question; and confessed by friends and enemies alike to be of a good and studious life, familiar with Hebrew, Greek, Latin, Italian, Spanish and French as well as his English, who better for the task? His Biblical scholarship, rather than coming firsthand, is derived from others; but why should he defer to learn from Luther, Erasmus, Ximenes and their like?

One lesson Tyndale perhaps gained from Erasmus is found in the preface to the latter's 1516 Greek New Testament:

> I totally dissent from those who are unwilling that the Sacred Scriptures, translated into the vulgar tongue, should be read by private individuals… And I wish that they were translated into all languages of all peoples, that they might be read and known, not merely by the Scotch and Irish, but even by the Turks and Saracens. I wish that the husbandman may sing parts of them at his plough, that the weaver may warble them at his shuttle, that the traveller may with their narratives beguile the weariness of the way.

This was plainly echoed by Tyndale about the year 1522 when he formed his resolve to translate. A Romanist clergyman told him that 'we were better without God's laws than the Pope's', to which Tyndale replied, 'I defy the Pope and all his

A typical printing press of the day

laws… If God spare my life, ere many years, I will cause a boy that driveth the plough shall know more of the Scripture than thou dost'.

Tyndale's skill in translation and his mastery of the English tongue was beyond compare. There was no English pattern to follow—John Wycliffe's work was too embroiled with the Vulgate text. Tyndale's English became the new minted coinage which all other 'traders' in the English Scriptures have needed to use. Words like 'genius', 'Saxon simplicity', 'tenderness', 'majesty', are now used in tribute: but not then! The book was denounced and Tyndale hunted.

Moving to Hamburg in 1529 he met Myles Coverdale again, good friend and helper. More editions and revisions, and parts of the Old Testament, were published in English, mostly in or around Antwerp. These editions con-

The 1536 Tyndale New Testament

firmed Tyndale's mastery and originality in the work of translation. Those able to compare noted that although Tyndale's other works show how deeply he had absorbed the theology of Luther, quoting and alluding to him, Tyndale's Biblical work, Old and New Testament, shows rather a growing clarity of commitment to the Biblical languages.

The Greek New Testament of Erasmus had been printed in 1516, 1519 and 1522, and it is evident that Tyndale used his third edition as the basis of his English version, and in this version is the acknowledged deposit laid of some ninety per cent of the vocabulary and form of later New Testaments, including the English New Testament of 1611. Let it not be forgotten that although in the Matthew's Bible Tyndale only officially supplied the Pentateuch and Jonah of the Old Testament, in an appendix to his New Testament he had translated various Old Testament passages for lectionary use and likely before his death gave his fuller Old Testament translations to Matthew's editor, John Rogers—and it is just as likely that Joshua to 2 Chronicles in Matthew's are directly from Tyndale's work. Regardless, all these passages show clear derivation from Hebrew, and not at all from Latin or Luther.

Spring 1535 arrived in Antwerp and so did Henry Phillips, who set about gaining Tyndale's trust. It was a trust gained by falsehood: Phillips' hope was of financial reward, and he set about to deliver Tyndale to those who sought him. By October 1536, Tyndale had been betrayed, imprisoned, strangled and burnt at Vilvoorde for Christ and His Word.[13]

Humble and irreproachable in his life, zealous and devoted in his work, beloved by his friends, respected by many of his enemies, faithful unto death: where among the army of martyrs shall we find a nobler than William Tyndale? Our English Bible, rooted in his work, is no dead piece of academic labour. It is the Word of God, transmitted through the agency of one to whom that Word was the very life of his soul.

2. COVERDALE

If Tyndale is justly styled 'Apostle of England', how shall we style Myles Coverdale? Too old to be a Timothy; better a Barnabas. Born near Middleham in the North Riding of Yorkshire, he became an Augustinian monk, ordained a priest in 1514 (at age twenty-seven) possibly at Norwich, and continued in the Austin monastery at Cambridge. Erasmus was at Cambridge from 1511 to 1514, so Coverdale may just have experienced at firsthand Erasmus' appeal to the authority of the Scripture text rather than to ecclesiastical tradition.

Coverdale certainly declared early for Christ and the Gospel. We have seen his involvement with Tyndale and others, and he seems to have been dedicated to Bible work from then on. After Tyndale's imprisonment Coverdale went on with the work, eventually supervising the production of the first complete Bible printed in English in 1535. This was probably done in Zurich, and as it attracted the attention of Cranmer, was dedicated to Henry VIII.

Henry VIII

Nowhere does Coverdale claim to have worked from the Biblical languages, but from 'fyue sundry interpreters' and 'sondrye translacions'. The five were probably Zwingli's German, Luther's German, Pagninus' Latin (a new and direct rendering from Hebrew in the Old Testament), the Latin Vulgate, and Tyndale. Another edition of the English Scriptures was begun in Paris around 1538, with Coverdale's supervision, but most of that edition was seized and burnt by the French authorities, a very few being sold. The type, and skilled workmen, were brought to London and Cranmer's Great Bible appeared in 1539, with the benefit of Coverdale's editorial labours and Thomas Cromwell's political protection.

The Dowager Queen Catherine Parr was sympathetic to the Reformation, and Coverdale, returning to England a year after the death of Henry, became her almoner,[14] and chaplain to the boy king, Edward VI. During Edward's reign, Coverdale was presented to the See of Exeter (August 1551), but was so poor that special arrangements had to be made for him lawfully to become bishop.

Myles Coverdale

Title page of Coverdale Bible

After Mary's accession to the throne in 1553 Coverdale was deprived and imprisoned. It seemed likely that he would be put to death—that was certainly the intention of the new Queen's administration. But by marriage he had become related to John Macalpine, chaplain to the king of Denmark, and that king intervened with Mary on Coverdale's behalf. Grudgingly he was released and permitted to go to Denmark.

Coverdale joined the growing company of English exiles on the Continent, at first with family in Denmark, then as chaplain to a group in Wesel, Germany. In August 1557 Coverdale was in Aarau with his wife and two children, and then from autumn 1558 to August 1559 he was in Geneva, serving as an elder of the English church under John Knox's pastorate! (He had already met Calvin on an earlier Continental trip.) There he preached and taught, but was soon caught up in Bible work once more.

With several fellow labourers including Christopher Goodman, William Cole and Calvin's son-in-law William Whittingham, he put forth that rugged version of the English Scriptures called the Geneva Bible.[15] This was the first English version to have verse numbers and, together with the explanatory notes, was a provision to earnest Bible searching. It is the Bible of the Puritans. More than thirty editions were printed in Elizabeth's reign, and it had the approval of Archbishop Parker and Bishop Grindal. It was the first English Bible to be widely available, and of handy size. The marginal notes aroused hostility within the Establishment, but they were a combination of scholarly help and popular observation: Protestant and Calvinistic. Italics were used to show interpolations,[16] and literal translations of awkward places were placed in the margins.

When Elizabeth came to the throne, Coverdale returned to England, and was involved in the consecration of Archbishop Parker in 1559. In common with many returning 'Mary-exiles', he was anxious for a much more thorough work of reformation than was pleasing to the English establishment. Although Coverdale had undertaken to 'be quiet' in his rectory at St. Magnus, London, he never conformed to the degree required of him, and resigned the living, but carried on a ministry whilst refusing to wear the surplice. His end was happy, we are told, and he died at the age of eighty-one, in 1568, having served the written and the Incarnate Word through four tumultuous reigns. His enduring exhortation, found in his Bible's 'A prologe to the reader', was, 'Go to now (most deare reader) & syt thee downe at the Lordes fete and reade his wordes'.

3. John Rogers and Matthew's Bible

John Rogers, minister, Bible translator and commentator, first English Protestant martyr under Mary I, was born in Deritend, Birmingham, *c.* 1500. He was educated at the Guild School of St John the Baptist and at Pembroke Hall, Cambridge, graduating B.A. in 1526. In 1534 Rogers went to Antwerp as chaplain to English merchants. He met Myles Coverdale, who led him to abandon the Roman Catholic faith, and William Tyndale. He there married Adriana de Weyden (anglicised to Adrana Pratt) in 1537. After Tyndale's death, Rogers pushed on with his predecessor's English version of the Old Testament—he used Tyndale as far as 2 Chronicles, taking Coverdale's 1535 translation for the remainder and for the Apocrypha.

The pseudonymous Matthew's Bible was published in 1537, printed in Paris and Antwerp by Sir Jacobus van Meteren, Adriana's uncle. Richard Grafton published the sheets with leave to sell the edition of one thousand five hundred copies in England. By Cranmer's influence the 'King's most gracious license' was granted to the version. In that same year the 1537 reprint of Myles Coverdale's translation had also been granted such a licence.

The pseudonym 'Matthew' is equated with Rogers, but it may be that 'Matthew' is a code for Tyndale's own name, too dangerous at that time to be openly employed. Rogers' actual share in that work involved translating the 'Prayer of Man-

The martyrdom of John Rogers 1555

34

asses' (inserted for the first time in a printed English Bible)[17] and general editing of the materials at his disposal. He also collated margin material from various sources, which notes are sometimes cited as a first English language 'commentary' on the Bible. Rogers also supplied the Song of Manasses for the Apocrypha, translated from a printed French Bible of 1535. Matthew's Bible was used in preparation of the Great Bible (1539–1540), antecedent of the Bishops' Bible, 1568, and of the Authorised Version.

John Rogers continued on the Continent and matriculated at the University of Wittenberg in 1540. He remained there for three years, a close friend of Philipp Melanchthon and other leading figures of the Reformation. After Wittenberg he spent four and a half years as superintendent of a Lutheran church in Meldorf, Dithmarschen, north Germany. He returned to England in 1548, and published a translation of Philipp Melanchthon's *Considerations of the Augsburg Interim*. He was made prebendary of St Paul's in 1550, where he was soon appointed divinity lecturer; however, he put aside the prescribed vestments, favouring instead a simple round cap.

On Mary's accession in 1553 he preached at Paul's Cross, commending the true doctrine taught in King Edward's days, and warning his hearers against pestilent popery, idolatry and superstition. Ten days later, on 16 August 1553, he was put under house arrest and deprived of his livings. In January 1554, Bonner, Bishop of London, sent him to Newgate Prison, where he was confined with John Hooper, Laurence Saunders, John Bradford and others for a year.

In December 1554 Parliament re-enacted the penal statutes against Lollards, and on 22 January 1555—two days after they took effect—Rogers with ten others came before the

Mary Tudor 1516-1558

council. A few days later, before Cardinal Pole's commission, he was sentenced to death. The crime? Denying the Christian character of the Church of Rome and the real presence in the sacrament. Denied a meeting with his wife, he awaited death cheerfully. He was burnt at the stake on 4 February 1555 at Smithfield.

Foxe's *Book of Martyrs* gives account of this first Marian Martyr, and should be read in full; but this following incident (taken from Foxe) lodged in the Protestant consciousness for generations:

> On the way he was met by his wife and his eleven children, one an infant in her arms. This sad sight did not move him, but he cheerfully and patiently went on his way to Smithfield, where he was burnt to ashes in the presence of a great number of people, and his soul ascended in a chariot of fire to that Redeemer of whom he was worthy, inasmuch as he loved him more than wife and children, yea, even than his own life also.[18]

4. John Frith (Fryth), 1503–1533

John Frith was born at Westerham, Kent, around 1503 (some say 1506) and educated at the local grammar school. He later went to Eton for two years, and then to Cambridge, Queen's College and then King's. By 1525 he was a junior canon at Wolsey's College, Oxford. Imprisoned for helping Tyndale, he was released in 1528.

The circumstances of John Frith's conversion are not recorded, but Tyndale, Frith and Barnes were together esteemed to be 'chiefe ryngleaders in these latter tymes of thys Church of England', and 'principall teachers of thys Church of England'.[19] The 'teachers' had no doubt as to their book, and the work upon which John Frith spent his energies—for such time as he had—was to continue to assist William Tyndale in the translation of the English Bible.

Since they had known each other in Cambridge, it is no surprise that Frith should seek out Tyndale when he too fled to Marburg in December 1528. As Tyndale laboured at the manuscripts, Frith was the production manager: dangerous work, overseeing the printing works, handling the sheets of forbidden matter. In this Frith relieved Tyndale, allowing him to concentrate on his replies to More and the ongoing translation work. Frith returned to England in 1532 only to be imprisoned, as much for his strong Protestant views of purgatory and the mass[20] as for his involvement with Scripture translation. Tyndale wrote warmly and appreciatively to the imprisoned Frith before his execution in the Smithfield fires in 1533.

These men, mighty under God—Tyndale, Coverdale, Rogers, Frith, companions in Christ, fellow-labourers in the Word even unto death—had carried the task of producing the Bible in our own tongue well towards maturity.

The burning of John Frith and fellow Protestant Andrew Hewit

Endnotes:

1. There was a paper mill in Strasbourg around 1430, just about the time that Gutenberg was there!

2. From a woodcutting in the British Museum (Harley mss., 5906b, no. 134).

3. The expression always used in bibliography for the very first one of its kind.

4. *Dictes or Sayengis of the Philosophres,* translated from French by the 2nd Earl Rivers.

5. It has been estimated that an early handwritten Bible on vellum might cost the price of a farm, a 16th-century printed Bible the price of a cow, and the price of a modern printed Bible the cost of a gallon of milk.

6. 'Possible', but the achievement of truly standard 'editions' of any printed text, including the Bible, was long in coming: see the later discussion of the printers and early printings of the Authorised Version.

7. That usage is not in favour now, but still has a lot to commend it.

8. At a trickle rate this had, inevitably, been going on since the Crusades, but now became a significant influence: this surge to Italy also explains why so many important Greek manuscripts came to rest in the Vatican, where Pope Nicholas V was an eager bibliophile (he left a library of five thousand items at his death).

9. There is difference of opinion as to Colet's competence in Greek at this point, or even whether he knew it at all! Researching this conflict has occupied a disproportionate amount of time. My conclusion was that he had some Greek, workable if not wonderful; able, if not adept.

10. People were so hungry to hear the Word of God in a language they could understand that within six months there were twenty thousand people packed in the church to hear him, and at least that many outside trying to get in!

11. There is still a main tourist site there in the 21st century. The press did in fact move about, not only in the Milan Duchy, but as far as Constantinople.

12. We can only mention in passing the huge labour of designing and casting the fonts for the new print technology. Typography has begun, and another area of creativity and beauty is helped into being through connection with the Scriptures.

13. There is a memorial to Tyndale in Vilvoorde, erected in 1913 by Friends of the Trinitarian Bible Society and the Belgian Bible Society. A bronze statue commemorating the life and work of Tyndale was erected in Victoria Embankment Gardens, London, in 1884, and another erected in 1866 on a hill at North Nibley, his supposed birthplace.

14. An almoner was the official who distributed alms or charity to those in need.

15. Strictly speaking, we should look at the Geneva (English) New Testament, published on its own first, but this was not the New Testament of the Geneva Bible.

16. Interpolation is the insertion of words into a text. In the case of the Scriptures, this is done to give the proper understanding of the Greek and Hebrew. These languages often omit words that are necessary in English, and so the English words have to be provided, although in italics to indicate their inclusion.

17. In understanding the insertion of the Apocryphal books in Holy Scripture, it must be noted that, although the Apocrypha was increasingly recognised by Protestants as outside the inspired text, it was still included in most Bibles—particularly those 'appointed to be read in Churches'—although generally in a group between the Old and New Testaments.

18. John Foxe, *The Book of Martyrs,* revised by W. Bramley-Moore (London: Cassell, Petter and Galpin, n.d.), p. 327.

19. *The whole workes of W Tyndall, Iohn Frith, and Doct. Barnes, three worthy Martyrs, and principall teachers of this Churche of England, collected and compiled in one Tome togither, beyng before scattered, and now in Print here exhibited to the Church. To the prayse of God and profit of all good Christian Readers* (London, 1573), quoted by Patrick Collinson, 'William Tyndale and the Course of the English Reformation', www.tyndale.org/ Reformation/1/collinson.html.

20. Among his judges at that time was the still unreformed Thomas Cranmer.

Chapter 4
ON TO HAMPTON COURT

BIBLE VERSIONS AND NEEDS: A QUICK REVIEW

yndale—along with Rogers and Frith—had sealed the English New Testament with his life in 1536. The various ensuing Coverdale editions, building on Tyndale and culminating in the Great Bible, were an integral part of Anglican worship. This is why the words 'appointed' and 'authorised' began to be associated with these versions. The need was for one appointed Bible to be used for congregational as well as personal reading; and the Anglican Church was, to its great credit, big on Bible reading! One agreed and approved Bible, to be read in copious portions day by day, and week by week—a Bible to become fixed in memory from generation to generation, common from family to family and parish to parish throughout the kingdom—this was the underlying desire.

Some of the reasons—constancy, continuity and wide familiarity—which supporters rightly urge today for the maintenance of the Authorised Version in common use and worship were among the very reasons for its appearance. Surely it follows that if there is to be one agreed Bible version in the church and nation, it had better be the best. Amongst the 'fiercer sort of protestants', as Elizabeth I had called them, the Geneva Bible of 1560 had become 'the best'. It was robust in translation, with strongly worded annotations; and it was portable, with the verses numbered. The Anglican establishment had caused the Bishops' Bible to be produced in 1568, attempting to wean away support from the Geneva, but it was a very lame production, with no possibility at all of securing general use.

At the risk of oversimplifying, I suggest just five significant steps over the nearly one hundred years from 1516 to 1611 which brought us to the Authorised Version: (1) the printed Hebrew (Bomberg 1517) and Greek (Erasmus 1516) texts;[1] then, English Bibles: (2) the Tyndale/Coverdale Bibles,[2] 1525ff; (3) the Geneva Bible (with Coverdale in the picture still), 1560; (4) the Bishops' Bible, 1568; (5) the Authorised Version of 1611. You may be surprised to see the Bishops' Bible included in these steps, but in the wisdom of God it became a crucial part of the road to the AV.

The Geneva Bible, and its swift acceptance amongst English Protestants, was highly disturbing to the ecclesiastical authorities.[3] Archbishop Parker put in hand a revision of the Great Bible, to be done by eight bishops and certain other scholars. Poor communication or lack of cooperation amongst the team led to a very uneven result, despite Parker's supposed general oversight. The Bishops' Bible, although 'appointed to be read in Churches', did not displace the Geneva Bible from all homes, studies, or even pulpits.

In Elizabeth's reign (1558–1603) there was already the draft of an act of Parliament addressing the need: 'An act for the reducing of diversities of Bibles now extant in the English tongue to one settled vulgar translated from the original.'[4] Nothing came of this in the reign of Elizabeth. Two years after the last printing of the Bishops' Bible in 1602, its manifest inadequacies were a large factor in King James' acceptance of the need for a new translation at the Hampton Court Conference of 1604. Sovereign providence had brought together the Biblical language texts, a newly mature English language and the technology of paper and print, and to the kingdom for just this hour men of urgent calling and ability in the way of Bible translation.

KING JAMES

England's last Tudor monarch, Queen Elizabeth I, had died at Richmond Palace, some way down river from Hampton Court, on 24 March 1603. Having reigned for forty-five years, she told Sir Robert Cecil, principal Secretary of State, a scant few hours before her death, '...a king shall succeed me; and who should that be but our cousin of Scotland?' James VI of Scotland became also James I of England, and the first to call himself King of Great Britain.[5]

Born in 1566, the son of Mary, Queen of Scots and her second husband, Henry Stewart (Lord Darnley), James became king of Scotland upon his mother's enforced abdication in 1567, when she was twenty-four, and he was thirteen months! No small part of the opprobrium attached to Mary was the suspicion of having been party to the murder of James' father. Ever a focus for Roman Catholic intrigue, she was imprisoned in England by Elizabeth I, and finally executed in 1587.

By the time that he entered England as king in 1603, at thirty-seven years old, James, the 'cradle Catholic' orphan-king, with both Stewart and Tudor connections through each parent, had experienced wholly Presbyterian influence and instruction, had subscribed to the Solemn League and Covenant, had publicly declared his admiration of the Scottish (Presbyterian) Kirk, and his dislike of the English (Episcopalian) liturgy.

On his accession to the English throne, James found the Protestant

James I

church in the kingdom divided. There were those who were in comfortable agreement with the ecclesiastical government and forms of worship established by law under Elizabeth I—generally we may say the Bishops' party; and there were those for whom the imposition of certain practices and forms caused distress of conscience, and who urged further reformation—the Puritan party. These latter welcomed the accession of James with some pleasure, anticipating that because of his upbringing he would be sympathetic to their cause and grant some relief of their grievances. Others would say, however, that as the nominee of Elizabeth, surely he would maintain her amazing balance of ecclesiastical powers under the Anglican umbrella. But then again, he was by birth a Roman Catholic Stewart, whose mother had been the child-bride of the Dauphin, later Francis II, King of France—perhaps the minority papal, continental party, could expect some crumbs from his table. Such expectations against such a background! Such power and opportunity against such an inadequate upbringing! Small wonder if James' character is hard to unravel. Small wonder if historians of differing partiality claim or denounce him according to selectively chosen aspects of his life and times.

THE MILLENARY PETITION

James' journey to London in 1603 became a triumphant royal progress, and he saw this exuberant welcome as a sign of God's approval and as tribute to him personally. He ingratiated himself with all as he went, distributing gifts, offices and titles, and appointing some three hundred new knights on his way south. The English were particularly pleased that the succession had been a peaceful one, as Elizabeth had no direct heirs.

Amongst those who met him on the way in April 1603 were some of the Puritan clergy, with a written statement of their complaints—their 'humble suit'. This was the 'Millenary' petition, supposedly from a thousand ministers, though in fact signed by not more than seven hundred and fifty. The main points urged in the petition were:

- The necessity of a trained preaching ministry of able men (and specifically the removal of those unfitted to preach a sermon at least every Lord's Day)

- The lawfulness of ministers' marriages

- Strict observance of the Lord's Day as a day of rest and prayer

- 'That men be not excommunicated for trifles and twelve-penny matters; that none be excommunicated without consent of his pastor.' (Let the church discipline the church!)

- Pluralism (ministers holding more than one living) to be outlawed

🙢 Popish ceremonies, garments and terms to be abolished ('no popish opinion…any more taught or defended')[6]

Hopes in the reforming party must have been high when James agreed that a conference should be held at Hampton Court on 1 November 1603 (later postponed). Given the desire that all should be 'agreeable to the Scriptures', it is no surprise that those same Scriptures should feature on the agenda of the conference. It is important to realise that everything and everybody involved in this anticipated conference was under the designation of Anglican, and thus Episcopalian, and of the 'one nation, one church' viewpoint. There were Anabaptists in Europe, but no Baptists nearer Hampton Court than Amsterdam! There were Presbyterians of the Geneva and John Knox heritage in Scotland, but scarcely yet in England. Tiny, harried and harassed 'separatist' meetings were appearing in East Anglia and London, forerunners perhaps of the independent churches of England and New England a generation later, but having no voice at all in the church affairs of James' kingdom.

BISHOPS AND PURITANS: A SHORT REMINDER

Along with the prevailing Anglicanism, it is also essential to know that for all their differences—and they were many—the bishops and the Puritans (and therefore almost all of the Authorised Version translators) were of a generally Calvinistic agreement in doctrine. Jacob Arminius' 'Five Points of Remonstrance'[7] against Dutch Calvinism were only declared in 1603 (and the echoing five point synopsis of the Calvinism of the Synod of Dordt was fifteen years away[8]). All the Puritans were Calvinists ('everybody knows that!'), but not all Calvinists were Puritans ('not many people know that!'). The Archbishop of Canterbury in 1603 was John Whitgift, strongly supportive of Episcopal principles and opposed to Puritanism, and yet was the author of the Calvinist Articles of 1595: he was perhaps the most thoroughgoing Calvinist ever to be Archbishop, but not at all a Puritan.

A Puritan family

The bishops were happy to maintain the Elizabethan status quo in every aspect of church and national life. The Puritans wanted further reform within the Anglican Church, edging towards Presbyterian form and government, and wanting less fuzzy

Archbishop Whitgift

42

doctrinal standards, with a Prayer Book that was more serviceable to piety—but still all within the 'Church of England'. In the course of another generation the hammer of Charles I on the anvil of Bishop Laud forged many Puritans into Nonconformists, forcing them to step outside of any adherence to the established church, but that is another story. At this point, bishops and Puritans were all (but only just!) Anglican and Calvinistic—as, necessarily, was the king. As they came to the conference neither the bishops nor the Puritans were satisfied with each other's preferred Bible version.

THE CONFERENCE

Now with some idea of the people who gathered, their anxieties, anticipations and agendas, we can look at the conference itself. On the first day, the king met the chief bishops, cathedral deans and his privy council, but with none of the Puritan party included. He discussed issues with the bishops, showing a certain amount of sympathy towards the requests of the Millenary Petition, and even expressing a willingness to make some changes in the English church. Bancroft, Bishop of London, and Archbishop Whitgift, argued for the status quo, cannily invoking Calvin's support in their pleadings with this Scottish-reared monarch. James wisely observed that in the course of some forty years (the length of the whole reign of Elizabeth) some corruptions might creep into any institution, civil or church.

The second day saw the leading Puritans, John Reynolds, Laurence Chaderton, John Knewstubs and Thomas Sparke, presenting their case for reform in the preaching, the liturgy and the Bible of the English church. John Reynolds was hugely concerned 'that there might be a new translation of the Bible, because those which were allowed in the reigns of King Henry the Eighth, and Edward the Sixth were corrupt, and not answerable to the truth of the original.'[9] To the dismay of the bishops, James seemed only too willing to hear, showing a great deal of understanding and accord. A programme to provide able preachers was as agreeable to the king as to Reynolds. A new translation of the Bible, framed from the Hebrew and Greek and to be published without notes, suggested by

The London of James I

43

Reynolds, was quite acceptable to His Majesty. However, when the Puritan scheme for church order revealed a Scottish-style Presbyterian model, the king became exasperated. He would have his bishops, and the bishops would have their king.

In the course of the third day of the conference, James again discussed issues with the bishops before the Puritan spokesmen were brought in. All, bishops and Puritans, were urged to be peaceful, obedient and temperate. Some Puritan requests were declined, and some that were then thought to have been agreed were never subsequently acted upon, or only partially accomplished. There was no real Prayer Book revision until 1662, by which time England was a very, very different place for Puritans.

In propounding their Presbyterian solutions to church order and national life the Puritans seem largely to have dissipated the general good will with which the king, intelligent and theologically aware, had received them. It was all a bit of an anticlimax, no real winners or losers. But—the new translation of the Scriptures was to be undertaken (the Geneva Version must be displaced somehow!), according to very direct instructions (see Appendix 1 to this book). The fruit of this labour, appearing in 1611, was to be the English version 'appointed to be read in Churches', and read by multitudes still to this day throughout the world. In the United Kingdom it has been usually referred to as the Authorised Version. Elsewhere it has more often borne the name of the king who presided at the Hampton Court Conference, and is the King James Bible.

THE COMMITTEES

James' declared intent to use all the talent, learning and experience which the bishops, universities, and clergy in general could supply to the work of a new translation was good. He wrote to Bancroft saying that he had appointed for the translation of the Bible 'certain learned men to the number of fifty-four, divers of whom had no ecclesiastical preferment'.[10] Bancroft was to write to the Archbishop of York and other bishops, in the king's name, persuading them to find any benefice, of the value of twenty pounds at least, that could be settled on one of those employed on the work of the translation. The bishops were also to be exhorted to identify in their dioceses those who were especially skilled in the Biblical languages, known for painstaking competence in dealing with hard places and misunderstandings of the Scripture. These were to make themselves known to committees and to communicate their own observations as called upon.

A flavour of the men of the committees is all that will be offered here, for the list of the labourers and their assigned portions of the Bible has been often published. The men included some of the most distinguished divines of that day, as well as others of whom history has preserved scarcely any remembrance. They were divided into six committees, two to meet in Oxford, two in Cambridge, and two in Westminster. (See the complete list in Appendix 4.)

The first committee of ten met at Westminster, to work on the Pentateuch and historical books as far as 2 Kings. Lancelot Andrewes, then Dean of Westminster, was president of this company; he was afterwards Bishop of Chichester, then Ely, and then Winchester. He died in 1626 and the preacher at his funeral said that Andrewes understood fifteen languages. Another in Andrewes' Westminster Committee was Dr. Adrian Saravia, a very learned Spaniard, who had been Professor of Divinity at Leyden University. He became resident in England, attracting the attention of Archbishop Whitgift, who appointed him successively as prebend at Gloucester, Canterbury, and Westminster. Spoken of as educated especially in many languages, he died in 1613. The Regius Professor of Hebrew and fellow of King's College, Cambridge, Geoffrey King, was at Westminster, as was William Bedwell of St John's College in the same university. Bedwell spent many years in preparing an Arabic lexicon, the commencement of a Persian dictionary, and an Arabic translation of the Epistles of John.

Lancelot Andrewes

The second committee, working with the Old Testament from Chronicles to Canticles, met at Cambridge. Their president was Edward Liveley, Regius Professor of Hebrew at Cambridge.

The third company met at Oxford to complete the Old Testament, from Isaiah to Malachi. Dr. John Harding, of Magdalen College, Regius Professor of Hebrew, and rector of Halsey, in Oxfordshire, was president of this company. Dr. John Reynolds, chief advocate on the Puritan side at the Hampton Court conference, was conspicuous among the Oxford translators as was Dr. Miles Smith, who afterwards wrote the preface.

A fourth committee, of eight members, also met at Oxford, working on the Gospels, Acts, and Revelation. Dr. Thomas Ravis, then dean of Christ Church, afterwards, successively, bishop of Gloucester and of London, was president. George Abbot, dean of Winchester but later better known as Archbishop of Canterbury from 1611, was

Archbishop Bancroft

THE AUTHORISED VERSION —

one of this Oxford group. Sir Henry Savile, tutor in Greek to Queen Elizabeth, provost of Eton College in 1596, and knighted by King James in 1604, also laboured in the New Testament committee.

Another group of seven assembled at Westminster, to translate the Epistles of Paul, and the general Epistles, with the sixth and last committee working on the Apocrypha at Cambridge. All told there were between forty-seven and fifty-four persons named at any time in the main lists of King James' translators; but others are also mentioned as engaged upon the version.

REVISION AND COLLATION OF THE COMMITTEES' WORK

1. Miles Smith's 'mere English'

This phrase, 'mere English', had been dear to Elizabeth I, using the word 'mere' in its primary, though now rare, meaning of 'pure, unmixed, exactly right'. She meant it of her loyal people, her triumphant sailors, her accommodating church. But in contemplating Bible translation labourers from Tyndale and Coverdale to Hampton Court, the phrase comes much to mind in connection with the English Bible. They pursued a 'mere English' Bible that was just right, pure and simple; in textual authority—from the Greek and Hebrew texts, the 'verities' as they were styled; in profusion and yet stability of copy—printed; and in accessibility—not the religious-authority tongue of Latin nor the elite-authority tongue of French, but the common English tongue.

The names and the distribution of tasks amongst the 1604–1611 translation committees are reasonably well known, but the overall finishing work of Miles Smith is often lost from view. Miles Smith was born in Hereford, son of a butcher, and educated at Oxford; he graduated B.A. in 1573, M.A. in 1576, B.D. in 1585 and D.D. in 1594. Wanting 'nothing but books', and of widely acknowledged humble demeanour, he nonetheless became chaplain of Christ Church, vicar of Bosbury, prebendary of Hereford Cathedral and of Exeter Cathedral, then rector of Hartlebury.

Dr. Smith earned a widespread reputation for his knowledge of ancient languages: Chaldaic, Syriac and Arabic were reportedly as familiar to him as his own native tongue. In that age of blossoming in the study of ancient languages, he probably engaged directly with the Scriptures in Hebrew and Greek, and only in English as need arose. His 1632 biographer gives the following story of an event at Evensong one day in Hereford Cathedral: 'Being requested by the dean of the same church to read the first lesson, he yielded thereunto, and having with him a little Hebrew Bible, he delivered the chapter from it in the English tongue plainly and fully to that learned and judicious auditory'.[11]

It is no surprise then that he was named to join the translators, and not only that, but he was one of two required at the end to supply the editor's role and examine the whole work for consistency and integrity—the task which Parker had signally failed to accomplish for the Bishops' Bible. We have it again from the 1632 biography: 'He began with the first, and was the last man of the translators in the work: for after the task of translation was finished by the whole number set apart for that business, being some few above forty, it was revised by a dozen selected ones of them, and at length referred to the final examination of the learned Bishop of Winchester and Doctor Smith, who happily concluded that worthy labour'.[12]

It is probably from Miles Smith that we have the page and chapter headings of the 1611 editions of the Authorised Version. We also learn that Dr. Smith 'was commanded to write a preface, and so he did in the name of all the translators, being the same that now is extant in our church Bible'.[13] This substantial manifesto gives a comprehensive, scholarly and robust review and justification of the task and methods of the translators. It abounds with memorable and relevant material; my own favourite is this—'But now what piety without truth? what truth (what saving truth) without the word of God? what word of God (whereof we may be sure) without the Scripture?'[14]

But the style of the preface is so different from that of the 1611 Bible, that I offer this sample of Miles Smith in the pulpit—hoping that you will agree with me that this is more the style of our beloved Bible, echoes of Tyndale, Coverdale and the Geneva Bible:

> …Our sins do threaten God's vengeance upon us, our consciences do accuse us, the law containeth matter of indictment against us; all the creatures of God which we have abused, all the calling of God which we have neglected, do witness against us. Hell opens her mouth wide, being ready to swallow us up. The world forsaketh us, our friends have no power to help us.
>
> What is to be done in this case? What shift shall we make, what place of refuge shall we fly unto? Only this, that the son of God became the son of Man to make us the sons of God; vile he became, to exalt us; poor, to enrich us; a slave to enfranchise us; dead, to quicken us; miserable, to bless us; lost in the eyes of the world, to save us. Lastly, partaker of our nature, of our infirmity, of our habitation, to advance us to his kingdom and glory, that is, to be unto us according to his name, Emmanuel, God with us. God to enlighten us, God to help us, God to deliver us, God to save us…'[15]

As with many of the 1611 translators, preferment followed, and Miles Smith became Bishop of Gloucester in 1612. Four years later there was a new dean of the Cathedral, William Laud, the rising opponent of Puritans and plain religion. What a difficult working relationship it must have been, but that is not a part of our account! Miles stood with his convictions, shared in measure by the 1611 translators. I think of him, with affection, as carrying the mantle of his namesake, Myles Coverdale, in these last miles on the road to the Authorised Version.

2. Resumé

The labours of the 1604 committees, editorially finished by Miles Smith, gave to the English-speaking world a printed, durable translation of the Scriptures, faithfully founded on the original language texts. Full use was made also of almost one hundred years' labour, drawing not only on English but other European languages, too. Certainly in the New Testament more than nine-tenths can be traced directly to Tyndale: down-to-earth and vigorous, with a directness of style owing so much to the initial wordsmith craftsmanship, under God, of Tyndale's vocabulary: educated, informed, but thoroughly Anglo-Saxon.

It is no surprise that of the eight thousand word vocabulary of the Authorised Version, words of Saxon derivation make up the same proportion, nine-tenths. Add to that the inescapable, unconscious seasoning of the stately rhythms of the Latin which was the working scholarly accomplishment of all these men, and the majestic, vibrant, persuading, insistently memorable cadences of the English Authorised Version are gone into all the world. The other great mother-tongue versions of the era were very much the works of one man, as with Luther's German and Karoli's Hungarian; our 1611 Bible is the work of one of a company of martyrs, taken and distilled, tried and tested, throughout the whole Reformation movement, and finally gathered in the committees of these learned men.

Regarding the choice of those eight thousand words, the translators themselves say:

> we have not tied ourselves to an uniformity of phrasing, or to an identity of words, as some peradventure would wish that we had done, because they observe, that some learned men somewhere, have been as exact as they could that way. Truly, that we might not vary from the sense of that which we had translated before, if the word signified the same thing in both places (for there be some words that be not of the same sense everywhere) we were especially careful, and made a conscience, according to our duty. But, that we should express the same notion in the same particular word; as for example, if we translate the Hebrew or Greek word once by *Purpose*, never to call it *Intent*; if one where *Journeying*, never *Travelling*; if one where *Think*, never *Suppose*; if one where *Pain*, never *Ache*; if one where *Joy*, never *Gladness*, etc.... We might also be charged (by scoffers) with some unequal dealing towards a great number of good English words. For as it is written of a certain great Philosopher, that he should say, that those logs were happy that were made images to

be worshipped; for their fellows, as good as they, lay for blocks behind the fire: so if we should say, as it were, unto certain words, Stand up higher, have a place in the Bible always, and to others of like quality, Get ye hence, be banished forever, we might be taxed peradventure with S. James his words, namely, *To be partial in ourselves and judges of evil thoughts.* Add hereunto, that niceness in words was always counted the next step to trifling, and so was to be curious about names too: also that we cannot follow a better pattern for elocution than God himself; therefore he using divers words, in his holy writ, and indifferently for one thing in nature: we, if we will not be superstitious, may use the same liberty in our English versions out of Hebrew and Greek, for that copy or store that he hath given us.[16]

Whatever popular opinion may now say about the English Authorised Version, there can be no doubt that it towers above all other works as a benchmark of 'mere English' Scripture. It is not in embellished courtly style: read the Dedicatory Epistle to James[17] for an easy comparison. It is not in the densely worded and complexly structured Establishment style: read the *Translators to the Reader* for comparison. It is not in the colloquial style: read a few scenes from Shakespeare for contrast. In this I intend no denigration of the material mentioned, but desire the outstanding quality of the 1611 English language Bible to be recognised as a signal gift of God, able to serve the saints and churches of God from generation to generation without being tied to passing styles, high or low. A slight misquotation from Shakespeare's *Julius Caesar* serves the Authorised Version well: 'Why, man, he doth bestride the narrow world like a colossus and we petty [versions] walk under his huge legs, and peep about to find ourselves dishonourable graves.'[18]

Spiritually it should be possible, without prejudice to other languages and peoples, to be profoundly grateful for the English tongue. Tyndale was not mistaken in his perception that the English of his day was wonderfully suited to render depths and shades of the Greek and Hebrew tongues. Arabic, for instance, a Semitic language, has a consonantal alphabet, leaving room for uncertainty of vowels, and frequently cannot transmit the more subtle nuances of Greek grammar. The Republic of Georgia has a relatively early New Testament, but by its nature it is difficult for the Georgian language to express many features of Greek syntax.

Remember, as you reach down your Authorised Version, that one of the infallible test questions for revealing 'heretics' in the Middle Ages was whether they possessed, or knew, any part of the Bible in their own language! The Waldensians and the Lollards suffered much from this procedure. As late as 1539 Thomas Forret was burnt outside Edinburgh Castle. Arraigned in court for teaching his congregation the Lord's Prayer and the Commandments in English, he had quoted the words of Paul from 1 Corinthians 14.19 in defence: 'Yet in the church I had rather speak five words with my understanding, that *by my voice* I might teach others also, than ten thousand words in an *unknown* tongue'. 'Where finds thou that?' his accuser cried. 'In my books, here in my sleeve', was the answer. The book, a Testament, was snatched from him and triumphantly waved at the court. 'Behold, Sirs, he has the heresy book in his sleeve— Know thou, Heretic, that it is contrary to our acts and express commands, to have a New Testament or Bible in English, which is enough to burn thee for'; which they then did.[19]

Truly, the accomplishment of the Scriptures in our own tongue, crowned in the Authorised Version of 1611, is marked with suffering and death, as well as diligent labour and extraordinary gifts: 'other men laboured, and ye are entered into their labours' (John 4.38). Thanks be unto God.

ENDNOTES:

1. There were others, of course, but these give a useful focus of dates for the gathering of what was to be the 'received' text.

2. I gather together Matthew's, etc., as one tranche with Tyndale/Coverdale.

3. And seemingly still is, as in this recent (1998) remark by an Anglican writer: 'The Bishops' Bible, [was] created by the Elizabethan hierarchy to avoid the use in church of the tendentious glosses of the Geneva, and its contentious translations…' (John Tiller, 'In the Steps of William Tyndale: Miles Smith as Bible Translator', *The Tyndale Society,* 6 October 1998, www.tyndale.org/TSJ/11/tiller.html).

4. *The National Archives,* Main Papers HL/PO/JO/10/1/1 1 Feb 1509 - 2 Mar 1581, www.nationalarchives.gov.uk/A2A/records.aspx?cat=061-hlpojo_1-1&cid=-1&Gsm=2008-06-18#-1.

5. Not strictly true until after the 1707 Act of Union.

6. 'The Millenary Petition 1603', *Hanover Historical Texts Project,* history.hanover.edu/texts/ENGref/er88.html, March 2001.

7. Arminius' 'Five Points of Remonstrance' are: (1) Free will or human ability: man has the ability to choose between good and evil in spiritual matters. (2) Conditional election: God's election is based on His foreknowledge. (3) Universal redemption or general atonement: Christ's sacrificial death was for all men, both those who will accept it and also for those who reject it. (4) The Holy Spirit can be effectually resisted in salvation. (5) Falling from grace: those who are truly saved can lose their salvation by falling from the faith.

8. The Calvinist response to the five points of Arminius are: (1) Total inability or total depravity: without the assistance of the Holy Spirit man cannot and will not choose good over evil. (2) Unconditional election: God's choice in election is solely on the basis of His sovereignty. (3) Limited atonement or particular redemption: Christ's sacrificial death was for the elect only. (4) Irresistible grace or the efficacious call of the Spirit: the drawing of men by the Holy Spirit to salvation cannot be rejected. (5) Perseverance of the saints: all who are truly redeemed will be kept in faith and persevere to the end.

9. Quoted by Joseph Robson Tanner, *Constitutional Documents of the reign of James 1, Parts 1603–1625* (London, England: Syndics of the Cambridge University Press, 1930), p. 63.

10. 'Preferment' in this context is the promotion to ecclesiastical office, which would provide finances. The translators had no ecclesiastical income!

11. How different from Tyndale's time, when, it is said, scarcely a handful in England had any knowledge of Hebrew; and how different from Colet's bold English readings scarcely one hundred years before! From Tiller 'In the Steps of William Tyndale', quoting Thomas Prior, *Sermons of the Right Reuerend Father in God Miles Smith, late Lord Bishop of Glocester. Transcribed out of his originall manuscripts, and now published for the common good* (London, England: Elizabeth Allde, 1632).

12. Ibid.

13. There is the delicious irony of all fourteen Scripture quotes in the preface being from the Geneva Bible, Smith's 'study' Bible. But until the Authorised Version was actually published, what else should he use?

14. *The Translators to the Reader* (London, England: Trinitarian Bible Society, 1998), p. 10.

15. Smith preaching on Isaiah 7.14, quoted by Tiller.

16. *Translators*, pp. 27–28.

17. The florid contribution of Thomas Bilson, Bishop of Winchester, not Miles Smith.

18. Act 1, scene 2, line 134, Cassius speaking of Caesar.

19. 'Persecution of the Bible', *Free Presbyterian Church of Scotland*, www.fpchurch.org.uk/News/view.php?id=26.

Chapter 5

Printing: techniques and problems

When discussing 17th-century printing there are important things to keep in mind, and, above all, we must avoid reading back into those times the technological achievements of consistency and stability that only began to be realised towards the end of the 19th century. The modern concept of an 'edition' of a printed work in which every copy of a print run of tens or hundreds of thousands would be identical, and in which a subsequent run of similar quantity would also be identical, was not in view five hundred years ago.

Print technology and aesthetics in England lagged well behind the best of Italy, France, or Holland, so that of over one thousand printers in Europe in the year 1500, there were only two in England, Caxton's old partner Wynkyn de Worde, and Richard Pynson. All of them suffered from a fundamental problem: as with manuscript copying, printing was a manual task. Accuracy depended upon the various 'hands on' operators in copy preparation, typesetting, proofreading, and so on. In a small print shop (and in England there were no others) all these activities could be happening together. Half a dozen operators might be making running changes, without any malice in mind, giving scope for what has been called 'piecemeal corruption' of the text. At any stage uncoordinated changes could be introduced, with the potential result of a day's output of printed sheets on the print shop shelves with differences between supposedly identical sheets. Those workmen were not being negligent,[1] for these were the familiar procedures of manuscript book production in the scriptorium,[2] but now the sheer quantity of printed sheets overwhelmed rudimentary control techniques. Additionally,

Cutting letters in a type foundry

should further sheets of that particular print run be required in, say, six months' time, the pages were no longer set up in type! No printer could afford to have lead type out of use, and so broke it up to be used for other pages or other documents as quickly as could be done.

In modern printing we expect a 'third printing' to be unchanged in any way from the first or the second; back then the next edition was in essence a starting all over again. Was the typesetting done from the same original manuscript? Or is the typesetter working from a now corrected manuscript? Is he working from pages of the previous print run, and which particular pages would they be? From Renaissance times to the Victorian era the most accurate copy one could have of any printed book would be one hand-corrected by the author![3]

A printing press with surrounding type cases, a similar setup to what would have been used in Caxton's day.

Doubtless, the translators of the Scriptures were delighted in the 'army of twenty-six lead soldiers' (printing with moveable type) which helped so much to propagate the Word of God.[4] But that would have often been coupled with dismay at the results of hasty printing. In reference to the 1541 reprinting of his German Bible, Luther wrote, 'For since they [printers] look only to their own greed they ask not how truly or falsely they have reprinted it. And I often found when I have read the reprinted edition that it is so garbled that in many places I have not recognised my own work, and have had to replace it.'[5]

Similar problems were built into the procedures for binding books, and once more we must put aside the ideas of modern practices. Books, including Bibles, would be stored as printed sheets or signatures[6] of such sheets. The printer or bookseller could sell them in that form to individuals who would arrange for their own binding, or the sheets would be bound up as books to order. But were the bound sheets all from the same day's print run, or even from the same printer?

The existence of printed copies of Bibles of a same date, such as 1611, but showing print or typographical differences between copies, is not surprising. Nor should it be distressing. This kind of editorial and 'technical' error is recognisable, well known, and amenable to correction—not the Word of God being corrected, but the mistakes of men in the process of production.

Along with all the general problems of book production in the 17th century, the sheer extent of the printed Bible must be remembered—almost eight hundred thousand words without Apocrypha, nearer one million words with Apocrypha included, as was generally the case in the official printings of the Authorised Version for two hundred and fifty years. This magnifies all the other difficulties involved—setting the type, manufacturing the paper, printing the pages, acquiring materials for binding, collating and binding the pages into a single volume.

Printing the Authorised Version

King Henry VII, who lived from 1457 to 1509, instituted the office of Royal Printer. Gutenberg died in 1468, when Henry was eleven years old, but William Caxton, 1422–1491, had set up a press in Westminster and printed the first book in England in 1477, when Henry was twenty and soon to be king. The new office of Royal Printer carried the right to print 'royal' material—statutes, proclamations, injunctions, and Acts of Parliament.

Early printed Bibles in English had been given just the normal privilege granted to a printer, a form of copyright supposed to protect the printer of one specific title from competition for a specific length of time. Once the Great Bible and then the Bishops' Bible were 'appointed to be read in the churches', a profitable market was open to the English book trade, and the right to print Bibles was shared within the Stationers' Company, the regulator of the book trade. The Crown (by then Elizabeth I) was glad to trade rights and monopolies, and some books became the exclusive printing right of individual printers.

Christopher Barker's printing device

When Christopher Barker became the Royal Printer in 1577 the office carried the right, or patent, to print all Bibles and Testaments, and the Book of Common Prayer. The patent was renewable and passed to heirs, and so it was that Christopher Barker's son, Robert, became responsible for the collation, revision, printing, and, more telling, the financing of the production of the Authorised Version, 1610–1611.[7]

The financing was a great burden, and commitment of the necessary capital was large and perilous. Partners had to be found to spread the printers' burden; work was 'subcontracted' and even the print shops themselves leased to the Stationers' Company to secure the needed funds. The company itself ran a peculiar cooperative scheme known as the English Stock (later the Bible Stock), which printed Bibles as well as other titles. Then, as now, new technology demanded financial outlay beyond the resources of most individuals or small companies, and there was fierce competition for the right to publish the most promising printed books.

Older publishing concerns were not content with a monopoly situation, and sought to overcome it. Cambridge University already had a 'perpetual' right to appoint three printers, to print 'all manner of books'. This dated from a charter of 1534, older than the Barker family patent, and Cambridge deemed that 'all manner of books' must include Bibles. A Cambridge Geneva Bible was printed in 1591, and a Cambridge Authorised Version in 1629. Oxford Bibles came later, in the 1670s.

The printer's 'master-piece' from Gutenberg to the 20th century, was the accomplishment of a large folio Bible, and when the manuscripts produced by the 1604 translation committees were finally delivered to the Barkers' premises in Aldersgate, work began on such a volume. The folio is one large sheet of paper, folded once, giving two leaves and four printable pages (using both sides).[8] The 1611 black letter Bible (see inset) took 366 folios, yielding 1,464 pages.

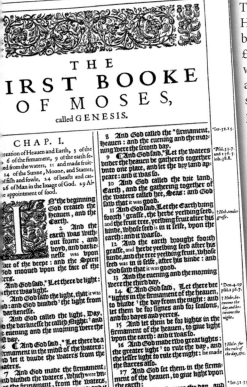

The 'He' Bible

In the light of our discussion of print shop problems in the previous paragraphs, you must not be surprised or dismayed to learn that there were differences in the printed text. A printer's error at Ruth 3.15 reading, 'he went into the city' instead of 'she went into the city' led to this first folio printing being known as 'the great He Bible'. Between 1611 and 1614 there were parallel streams of Authorised Version Bibles printed, distinguished as 'He' Bibles and 'She' Bibles. It seems that simultaneous printing was carried out in separate print shops, each using an exemplar in a different state of correction, or even a printer making 'corrections' as he went.

There were more mistakes than the He/She classic. Records of these Bibles being purchased give prices between £2-13-4 (£2.66) and £2-18-0 (£2.90), which in equivalent value today would be around £212.00: then it equated to six or seven weeks of a craftsman's pay, the price of a cow or several sheep. A black letter New Testament also appeared in 1611, followed in 1612 by a folio edition printed in roman type, fifty years after the example of the Geneva Bible in 1560. This 1612 printing did correct some of the errors of 1611.

John and Thomas Buck issued a folio edition of the Authorised Version at Cambridge in 1629, after the 1534 Henry VIII charter had been ratified by Charles I. Amongst those who prepared this Bible for the press were two of the original translators, John Bois and Samuel Ward: they were diligent in seeking to remove print errors of every kind, attending to punctuation and italics as well as the more usual issues. In 1638 a further Cambridge revision was printed, once again with

1611 black letter Bible

the editorial help of Bois and Ward. Revision in this context should not be linked with the later business of textual criticism and alteration, but rather the very needful labour of seeking an established printed text, free from the mechanical and editorial errors mentioned above.

Another significant Cambridge printing came in 1762, prepared by F. S. Paris and H. Therold, still pursuing the task of standardising spelling, punctuation, use of italics, and marginal annotations. Soon after that came the Oxford printing of 1769, Benjamin Blayney's careful completion of the work begun in the Paris Bible of 1762. This 1769 'Paris–Blayney' edition of the Authorised Version has remained the standard from that day to this.

A blind following of certain 'King James Version only' advocates[9] must ignore the issues of Bible production outlined here, and brush aside the question seriously important for them, of 'which particular 1611 Bible?' We should rather be very glad that inspiration and authority are neither made, nor broken, in the print shop, and very glad of those who have laboured to establish, settle and maintain the printed text of the translation work of the 1604 committees.

ENDNOTES:

1. Although as profit became an issue some were. The printer's bane, then as now, was pirate printings, aimed only at quick financial returns and careless of quality.

2. The long-acquired techniques of quality control in multiple manuscript hand-copying were, and still are, astounding, recalling the Masoretic procedures of Hebrew copying. These could not be applied to the new technology: the same long process of acquiring such control had to take place. It took centuries.

3. Notice the lists, amounting at times to pages, of 'errata' abounding in books printed before the early 20th century.

4. This idea has been attributed to everyone from Martin Luther and Gutenberg to Benjamin Franklin and Karl Marx.

5. English translation from *The Cambridge History of the Bible,* 3 vols., S. L. Greenslade, ed. (Cambridge, England: Cambridge University Press, 1975), 3.432.

6. A 'signature' is a group of consecutive pages normally made up from folded sheets.

7. The office of King's Printer was later to pass to his eldest son, another Christopher.

8. A similar page folded twice would give four leaves (hence quarto) and eight printable pages, and so on.

9. The King James Version only movement as a whole teaches that the Authorised (King James) Version is directly inspired by God and thus inerrant. Some of the more extreme members of the movement teach that the Greek and Hebrew texts should be corrected according to the AV, and that a person cannot be truly saved unless it is through the AV.

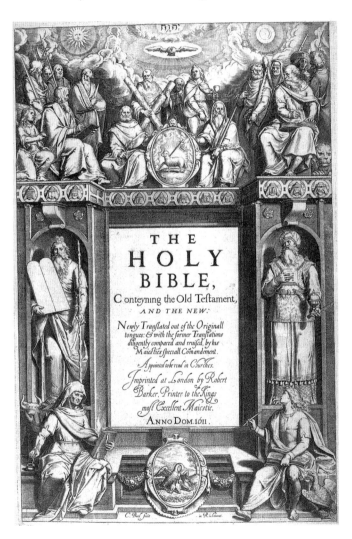

Title page to the 1611 first edition

Chapter 6

THE LAST CHAPTER?

The Authorised Version—the last chapter?

 he speed with which the late 19th- and 20th-century English-speaking world, Christians very much included, deserted the Authorised Version and its textual foundations is quite startling. This was especially so in the second half of the 20th century, when 'new', 'improved', and, always, 'better' versions, undergirded with strong commercial salesmanship, appeared regularly and found a ready market. A wholly deficient yardstick became accepted—that 'easy-to-read' is the same as 'easy-to-understand'—a frighteningly deceptive approach to any serious reading, and much more so in connection with the Scriptures. So much has this become the rule that the very nature of the Scriptures is mostly ignored, or even held against them.[1] We have the Word of God in a wealth of manuscript testimony; honest use of that testimony and rigorous translation of the text are of greater importance than 'market needs'.

The year 2009 saw great celebration of Darwin's theories; those mistaken theories one hundred and fifty years earlier had a thoroughly debilitating effect on both scholarly and popular views of the Bible. The Reformers had accepted the simple integrity of the Bible witness, but by the 19th century the Bible had come to be regarded as just another literary text, without inherent authority or meaning. Darwin's theories led 19th-century 'experts' to apply evolutionary methodology to the Bible, at every level. The picture of Scripture as an imperfect record of the religious seeking of primitive mentality, moving through to more highly evolved views, gave a way of reading the Bible which completely destroys its authority. This was not accomplished without a 'scholarly' manipulation and reinterpretation of textual and translation issues, and many of the modern Bible versions are built upon these sandy foundations.

When we consider the trail of the early printed English text of the Bible, we gain a partial insight into the astounding nature of textual preservation under the providences of Almighty God. This one thread—the printed English text derived from Greek and Hebrew sources—appeared. It then appeared in almost simultaneous 'rival' editions.[2] It appeared in noble style.[3] It appeared in hurried and careless style.[4] It appeared in editions which were wrought in concern for the glory of God and for the work of the Gospel.[5] It appeared in editions which were for utterly controversial exercise.[6] It appeared in editions which were pirated for filthy lucre.[7] Very rarely did it appear as a 'pure' translation from the Biblical languages, but often showing the influence of Latin and German. It was both helped and hindered by editors and arrangers of varying quality. Yet, in all of this we see the sovereign purposes of

God, whereby all things truly work together beyond the limited perception or arrangements of men, to accomplish the preservation, settling and transmission of the Scripture of Truth.

The very nature of the Bible demands an exercise of faith and discernment, indeed so much so that we can expect such heretical attitudes towards the Scriptures as those mentioned by the Apostle Paul in 1 Corinthians 11.19, 'there must be also heresies among you, that they which are approved may be made manifest among you'. Our 1611 Bible is the fruit of the work of a company of martyrs and diligent labourers, accomplished and distilled, tried and tested, throughout the whole of the Reformation and Puritan times. Then it was gathered in the committee work generated by the Hampton Court Conference.

Let us, however, never be so satisfied with our perception and choice of the printed text of Scripture, that we fall short of the exercise of faith in Jesus Christ and Him crucified, which is the blessed voice of all the Scripture: '...but these are written, that ye might believe that Jesus is the Christ, the Son of God; and that believing ye might have life through his name' (John 20.31).

A word about the Hampton Court king, James VI of Scotland and I of England

Given his background and upbringing[8] it is small wonder that James' character is hard to unravel. It is not strange that historians of differing partiality claim or denounce him according to selectively chosen opinions of his life and times. I hesitate to enter the controversies about James' morals. Such matters are even less relevant to the nature of the AV than David's murderous adultery is to the nature of the Psalms.

Perhaps the English king was indiscreet in his display of affection; perhaps he was of unprepossessing appearance. Perhaps he has suffered, as the Conference itself has suffered, from the 'everybody knows...' syndrome, when in effect nobody knows but many say so on the slender authority of increasingly hostile comment. Do those, for instance, who leeringly relish the portrayal of James leaning on his young men, take into account that his lower limbs were deformed and in need of support from childhood? That of course proves nothing, any more than the insidious struggles of a modern sex-obsessed society, determined to leave no character unturned, prove the opposite. As Titus tells us, 'unto the pure all things *are* pure: but unto them that are defiled and unbelieving *is* nothing pure; but even their mind and conscience is defiled' (1.15). We note sadly in passing that the attack on opponents' character has long been a favourite and leading weapon with the less thoughtful supporters of the Received Texts and

King James I

59

the Authorised Version, who prefer mud to integrity, and who should not complain if the weapon is used against their views in similarly unprincipled ways.

Authorised

Usage in Britain from the beginning settled in the naming of this Bible as the Authorised Version, and apart from many other considerations this does avoid the (misleading) figurehead connection with King James I of England (James VI of Scotland). People challenge the use of the word 'authorised' as lending a spurious *gravitas* to this Bible, and tell us, somewhat patronisingly, that there has never been any record found of the 'authorising' of the 1611 publication. But this is to ignore the history and avowed purpose of the English Bible.

Coverdale's and Matthew's Bibles had both been 'licensed' (approved for printing) in 1537, and the Great Bible of 1539 was the first to have the wording 'Appointed to be read in Churches' on the title page. Next came the Bishops' Bible in 1568, and in the TBS Library is a 1585 copy of this, with 'Holy Byble…authorised and appointed to be read in churches' on the title page. However strange this may appear to a modern self-styled democratic society, there was concern that what was to be read aloud in churches, in copious portions, as the mirror of Christ, rule of life and ground of ministry, had some provenance beyond the personal choice of every reader (would that it were so still).

Now, in 1604, Directive Number 1 from James to the translators reads—'The ordinary Bible read in the church, commonly called the Bishops' Bible, to be followed, and as little altered as the original will permit'[9]—so who will deny the right of the 1610–1611 printers to reproduce the earlier title page? It neither imposed nor imparted any strange kingly, governmental or priestly power to the text, but it assured all ministers, readers and hearers of that time that this was the agreed Bible text.

Explicit in the style 'Authorised Version' is the recognition of the need for, and the provision of, a standard Bible text—a matter lost sight of almost completely in the disputes of recent decades (centuries?), but achingly needing to be addressed and reclaimed. The lack of one recognised Bible version, in regular and familiar use amongst English-speaking Christians, creates a serious distress and disjunction in Christian affairs. None of the myriad versions which have been put forward for the job from 1885 onward even look like coming anywhere near the leader of the previous two hundred and fifty years—indeed some have already fallen from use and knowledge, whilst the Authorised Version maintains its course, reputation and usefulness.

English?

William Tyndale is famously quoted as saying to a priest of his time, 'If God spare my life, ere many years, I will cause a boy that driveth the plough shall know more of the Scripture than thou dost'. This is some-

Woodcut showing ploughing with oxen

times brought forward as an argument **against** the English of our Authorised Version, as being, men say, so obviously 'untrue'. 'How well educated were 16th-century ploughboys?' we are asked. This ignores two things. First, from Tyndale's days until within the last century, there are well attested accounts of the simplest unlettered people, with a hunger for an understanding of the Word of God, teaching themselves to read, using only the English Bible as their textbook. Second, the Bible in Tyndale's English would be more widely and more plainly read aloud and preached from, as in Nehemiah 8.8: 'So they read in the book in the law of God distinctly, and gave the sense, and caused *them* to understand the reading'. By such hearing, even the unlearned ploughboy could attain a better knowledge of the Scriptures than the foolish priests, and might even be moved to learn to read for himself so that he could search the Scriptures.

We speak of Tyndale's English, and his goal was that of Wycliffe: a translation of the Bible into English that anyone could understand. He did not want the Bible limited to educated clergymen, using terminology which would have been beyond the average farm labourer. At the same time, however, as ably illustrated by his work, Tyndale was not interested in translating the Scriptures into 'street' language. The Scriptures were special, and deserved more than the flat, unmelodic, often coarse language used in everyday vernacular. Tyndale knew that the ploughboy of his day would not have been educated, but that ploughboy was able to understand (or intelligent enough to learn) more than simple 'farm lingo'; Tyndale's translation reflects this middle ground.

The translators of our Authorised Version explicitly confirm this approach, declaring: 'Lastly, we have on the one side avoided the scrupulosity of the Puritans… as also on the other side we have shunned the obscurity of the Papists… But we desire that the Scripture may speak like itself, as in the language of Canaan [i.e., the common speech of the Israelites], that it may be understood even of the very vulgar'.[10] Their desire was to make one principal good translation, 'not justly to be excepted against; that hath been our endeavour, that our mark':[11] to have one translation for use in castles, churches and homes, to be read, preached and profited from.

The theology and the style of the Scriptures would be mutually supportive in communicating the words of God, as described by Prof. A. Cook:

The translators of the Authorized Version endeavoured, out of the English renderings with which they were acquainted, compared with the originals and the principal versions into other tongues, ancient and modern, to frame one which should surpass them all by appropriating the chief excellences of each—so far, at least, as these excellences could be harmonized with one another. In so far as it did thus reconcile pre-existing differences, it became a powerful agent in establishing unity throughout the English nation.[12]

Standing on the shoulders of those who had gone before, in English as well as in other languages, the 1604 committees had great advantage. 'The Authorized Version profited by all the controversy regarding previous translations. Practically every word that could be challenged had been challenged.'[13] Thus, the AV displayed the best of the best, while avoiding the pitfalls of previous translations.

Furthermore, the language of the AV was not that of new words; rather, it was based on those of Tyndale. Nor was it introducing new styles of phrasing, being based soundly on the Greek and Hebrew of the Biblical texts. The AV was rendered in a form of language that rose above advantages of wealth or social standings, and was—as with other classics of English literature—not limited to the language of a specific time period. This language is not strictly of the 17th century, as can be readily seen, for instance, by Shakespeare's use (or misuse) of the pronouns 'thee' and 'thou'; these the AV translators consistently used to distinguish the singular and plural pronouns, as differentiated throughout the Greek and Hebrew texts, in an effort to convey more accurately the true sense of those texts.

However, even through the first one hundred years following the publication of the Authorised Version, some were calling for updating. To this Jonathan Swift replied,

> It is Your Lordship's Observation, that if it were not for the *Bible* and *Common Prayer Book* in the vulgar Tongue, we should hardly be able to understand any Thing that was written among us an hundred Years ago: Which is certainly true: For those Books being perpetually read in Churches, have proved a kind of Standard for Language, especially to the common People. And I doubt whether the Alterations since introduced, have added much to the Beauty or Strength of the *English* Tongue, though they have taken off a great deal from that *Simplicity*, which is one of the greatest Perfections in any Language. You, My Lord, who are so conversant in the Sacred Writings, and so great a Judge of them in their Original, will agree, that no Translation our Country ever yet produced, hath come up to that of the *Old and New Testament*: And by the many beautiful Passages, which I have often had the Honour to hear Your Lordship cite from thence, I am persuaded that the Translators of the Bible were Masters of an *English* Style much fitter for that Work, than any we see in our present Writings, which I take to be owing to the *Simplicity* that runs through the whole.[14]

One hundred and sixty years further on, in 1870, even as scholars were anticipating a revision of the Authorised Version, Ellicott encouraged them to 'limit the choice of words to vocabulary of the present [Authorised] version, combined with that of the versions, that preceded it; and in alterations preserve as far as possible the resonant cadence of the Authorized Version'[15]—that despite the Authorised Version translators having chosen a mere eight thousand English words with which to render the full body of inspired Scripture.[16]

One reason for retaining the Authorised Version's language and diction even into the 21st century is the influence the AV has had on the vast body of literature in English. Those works now regarded as classics bear the hallmark of the AV's style, and many words and phrases from the AV have crept into not only literature, but everyday speech. Many have escaped by the skin of their teeth (cf. Job 19.20); many a man's daughter is the apple of his eye (cf. Psalm 17.8). Many are familiar with the Nativity event recorded in Luke 2, and would find any alterations to the familiar phrases of the Authorised Version foreign and unpleasant to the ear.

Cook notes that it is not just as literature that the AV has made its impact. More importantly, we see throughout later writings that the themes and language of much of literature—taken from the AV—are Scriptural, and quotations from and allusions to the Bible, and particularly from the AV, are used even in highly secular works, although often the source is not acknowledged—the authors assume the reader will recognise the source. Cook sums it up like this: 'The elevation and nobility of Biblical diction, assisted by its slightly archaic tinge, have a tendency to keep all English style above meanness and triviality'.[17]

Even a leading 21st-century atheist agrees with that. Richard Dawkins, being asked why he wanted to participate in the 2011 celebrations of the Authorised Version, replied 'You can't appreciate English literature unless you are steeped to some extent in the King James Bible, people don't know that proverbial phrases which make echoes in their minds come from this Bible. We are a Christian culture, we come from a Christian culture and not to know the King James Bible, is to be in some small way, barbarian'.[18]

However useful and appealing and encouraging much of our information is, it does not directly respond to the cry of someone, say in secondary education, who finds the AV 'hard to read'. There are three issues to address: (1) vocabulary: the meaning of single words; (2) sentences and paragraphs: what are the strings of words actually saying? and (3) spiritual matters.

⚘ **Vocabulary.** In connection with vocabulary there is a general rule: if a word is not understood, find out the meaning! Ask; inquire. Consult a general dictionary (online searches are very good for this). Look in a Bible dictionary. Ask a parent, a pastor or other church leader. A few questions will settle the understanding of a word for ever in your mind; and after all, the vocabulary of our English Bible is by no means extensive. We are told that Shakespeare used from fifteen to twenty thousand different words, and the Hebrew Old Testament and the Greek New

Testament have their own distinct vocabulary. Our English Authorised Version's eight thousand different words comprise a surprisingly small vocabulary, and most of the words are short, averaging little more than four letters. (Yes, we know about Mahershalalhashbaz, for instance, at Isaiah 8.1, but asking, as suggested above, should reveal that it is not an English word, but a transliteration of four Hebrew words, left in that form to draw attention to the meaning of the name 'swift is the booty, speedy the prey' when Damascus and Samaria were about to be engulfed by Assyria.) It is a great advantage of the AV that the vocabulary will not change with passing trends.

§ **Sentences and paragraphs:** the meaning of a connected sequence of words. In this, it is well to settle one matter first: the Bible is not 'divinity for dummies', it is not a novel or a fictionalised documentary. Rather 'all scripture *is* given by inspiration of God, and *is* profitable for doctrine, for reproof, for correction, for instruction in righteousness' (2 Timothy 3.16).

Scripture is profitable—useful, of great reward and benefit—and it expects a level of effort in realising that profit. Quoting the Bible again, consider Acts 17.11: 'These were more noble than those in Thessalonica, in that they received the word with all readiness of mind, and searched the scriptures daily, whether those things were so'. These noble Bereans 'received the word'—we might almost say 'they went to meet it', and accepting the obligations of the Word of God they did so 'with all readiness of mind'. It was to be thought about. And then they searched, examined, sifted, questioned (and remember that this was no 'modern' version—they did not have the 'Berean Searcher's Study Bible in Easy Macedonian'[19]).

They had a willingness to take time to search the Scriptures, to interrogate the text; and this is key to solving many difficulties. Persevering use of the references to other parts of the Bible, seen in the centre or side columns of a Bible page, will often yield insight for meaning. Asking questions works well here also, especially when you remember that this is not storing up exam facts, but desiring to learn (doctrine and reproof), expecting to be changed (correction, instruction in righteousness).

§ **Spiritual matters:** Understanding the 'sentences and paragraphs' leads us on to spiritual matters, which really falls outside the scope of this paragraph, but must be mentioned. In John 5.39 Jesus speaks to the Jews saying, 'Search the scriptures; for in them ye think ye have eternal life: and they are they which testify of me'. It was almost sarcastic: nobody searched the Hebrew Old Testament and its Greek translation, the Septuagint, as thoroughly as these Jewish leaders did. But they did not look for, and did not find, the chief Person and the principal matter of the Scriptures, the Lord Jesus Christ, and thus did not find eternal life in Him.

§ **And finally, just one longing, yearning cry of my own:** more and greater preaching of this blessed English Authorised Version would go far to resolving these difficulties.

The language and style of the English Authorised Version are timeless, not limited to 1611 but rooted in and derived from translations such as Tyndale, Coverdale, Geneva, Bishops'; not limited to 1611 but becoming our lingual 'house style', the basis of English literature for centuries to come. As with the classics of English literature, speaking not only to their own generations but also to those of a later time, words were carefully and thoughtfully chosen and placed, so as to convey the Word of God to all who would hear, 'mark, learn and inwardly digest':[20] the king in his palace, the housewife, the cleric, the shepherd, the lawyer, the beggar, and these not only in 1611 but also in 1711 and 1811 and 1911, and now in 2011.

An unfinished story

The few pages of this book should suffice to show a wonderful story—the Authorised Version from 1611, the Word of God and Scripture of Truth in English. Others for 2011 will make much of the cultural and linguistic heritage of our Authorised Version,[21] and we are not unmindful of these riches of Divine Providence. However, as we dwell on the living, ongoing and unfinished spiritual usefulness of the AV, please do think on these things:

IT IS **DEPENDABLE.** The textual basis and principles of translation of the Authorised Version are openly known and settled; it will not change under your hand as the smoke screens of 'best manuscripts' and 'meaningful vocabulary' are used to make room for yet one more new version.

IT IS **MEMORABLE.** There is in the regular reading, especially aloud, of the Authorised Version an almost inescapable tendency for the words to linger in the memory—which does not seem to be the case for the more recent renderings into English of the text of Scripture. What fruit this 'self adhesive' quality of the AV yields to those who actually apply themselves, with the spirit and the understanding, to memorising Scripture and 'bringing into captivity every thought to the obedience of Christ',[22] is a great good beyond measure.

IT IS **AVAILABLE:** widely available in general bookshops, Christian bookshops, and many other sources, in so many sizes, styles and bindings and prices.

IT IS **IN USE!** The Authorised Version is no museum piece, but a regular part of life in homes, churches and colleges, in large quantities. Many evangelists, missionaries and preachers still make preference of the AV. In current[23] worldwide sales figures of Bibles, the Authorised Version is listed second, after the NIV, both on monetary figures and quantities. If we could figure in the production, distribution and use of Bibles in other languages which rejoice in the same pedigree as the AV, there is no telling what the numbers might be. Then add the quantities which are granted free of charge to those who ask, and the copies distributed during earlier decades of its four hundred year reign—the numbers would be staggering.

Not only is the AV in use, it is blessed in use! Comparisons with other versions are not here attempted, only the squashing of the 'God can't/won't use that old thing' remarks. Souls are being called and saved; congregations are being nurtured; lives and families are being directed in holiness: all under the strong spirit and good hand of God in the faithful use of the Authorised Version. The last chapter of our book this may be—but it is nowhere near the last chapter of the wonderful and unfinished story of the Authorised Version.

ENDNOTES:

1. Wouldn't it have been better, people say or imply, if the Holy Spirit of God should have caused the Scriptures to be written in a linear, chronological, even topical style? They would prefer anything but the sixty-six book series of overlapping and integrated accounts of the history of redemption, needing prayerful searching and the use of help (Acts 8.31) and still, even in the 21st century, best grasped when well read, aloud.

2. It then appeared in almost simultaneous 'rival' editions, e.g., Geneva and Douay-Rheims.

3. It appeared in noble style: a 1612 copy now found in the University Library in Heidelberg once belonged to Elizabeth, daughter of James I. It is bound in fine calfskin and has the royal arms of the king and his Stuart descendants stamped in gold on the front cover.

4. It appeared in hurried and careless style: one 1611 AV printed had 'Judas' for 'Jesus' in Matthew 26.36, and a 1612 printing had 'scorners' for 'sorcerers' in Revelation 22.15.

5. It appeared in editions which were wrought in concern for the glory of God and for the work of the Gospel; e.g., a roman-script edition of the AV (rather than the hard-to-read black letter—see Appendix 2) was printed in 1616. By 1620 the first annotated edition of the AV appeared with a document entitled *The Way of True Happiness…By Questions and Answers opening briefly the meaning of euery seuerall Booke and Chapter of the Bible… appended.*

6. The Bible appeared in editions which were for utterly controversial exercise, e.g., Douay-Rheims (or Rheims-Douai), a Roman Catholic translation, was first published in 1609.

7. It appeared in editions which were pirated for filthy lucre: by 1625 printers in Amsterdam were printing copies of the AV, and a printing is alleged to have taken place in the American colonies in 1752 in an effort to bypass the royal edict that Bibles only be published in Britain.

8. As mentioned in chapter 4, James' life had been a mixture of Roman Catholic and Presbyterian, Stewart and Tudor, at a time of upheaval in many aspects of British life, and the monarch would be branded as saint or sinner depending upon the philosophy or whim of the author.

9. See Appendix 1, 'The 1604 Directives'.

10. *The Translators to the Reader: The Preface to the Authorised Version of 1611* (London, England: Trinitarian Bible Society, 1998), p. 28.

11. Ibid., p. 24.

12. Albert S. Cook, *The Authorized Version of the Bible and Its Influence* (London: G. P. Putnam's Sons, 1910), p. 50. Cook was Professor of English language and literature at Yale University. This book was originally a chapter in volume 4 of *The Cambridge History of English Literature*.

13. Ibid., p. 51.

14. Jonathan Swift, *A Proposal for Correcting, Improving, & Ascertaining the English Tongue* (London: Benjamin Tooke, 1712), p. 493, on *Corpus of Electronic Texts: a project of University College Cork*, www.ucc.ie/celt/online/E700001-017.html.

15. Quoted in Cook, p. 65.

16. This compared with the one hundred and twenty thousand entries in the 1990 *Concise Oxford Dictionary of Current English* (R. E. Allen, ed., 8th ed. Oxford: Clarendon Press, 1990).

17. Cook, pp. 78–79.

18. *The 2011 Trust*, 'Richard Dawkins lends his support to 2011 Trust', 19 February 2010; www.2011trust.org/news/q/date/2010/02/19/richard-dawkins-lends-his-support-to-2011-trust.

19. The noble Bereans 'received the word', doubtless studying the Hebrew Old Testament in synagogue and Greek Septuagint in less formal settings, rather than anticipating the modern tendency to focus on other writings for their spiritual insight. They did not need modern 'easy-to-read' translations or study Bibles but instead dug into the meat of the Word and let Scripture interpret Scripture.

20. From the collect in the 1662 Book of Common Prayer for the 2nd Sunday in Advent.

21. Richard Dawkins has the effrontery to declare that Christians must not be allowed to 'hijack' these aspects of our treasured Bible! *The 2011 Trust*.

22. See 2 Corinthians 10.5.

23. Christian Booksellers Association, June 2010; www.cbaonline.org/nm/documents/BSLs/Bible_Translations.pdf.

APPENDIX 1:

THE 1604 DIRECTIVES

Here is a succinct directive as to principles and procedures from the king to the translators.

1. The ordinary bible read in the church, commonly called the bishops' bible, to be followed, and as little altered as the original will permit.

2. The names of the prophets, and the holy writers, with the other names in the text, to be retained, as near as may be, accordingly as they are vulgarly used.

3. The old ecclesiastical words to be kept, viz. as the word church, not to be translated congregation, &c.

4. When any word hath divers significations, that to be kept which hath been most commonly used by the most eminent fathers, being agreeable to the propriety of the place and the analogy of faith.

5. The division of the chapters to be altered either not at all, or as little as may be, if necessity so require.

6. No marginal notes at all to be affixed, but only for the explanation of the Hebrew or Greek words, which cannot, without some circumlocution, so briefly and fitly be expressed in the text.

7. Such quotations of places to be marginally set down, as shall serve for the fit reference of one scripture to another.

8. Every particular man, of each company, to take the same chapter or chapters; and, having translated or amended them severally by himself, where he thinks good, all to meet together, to confer what they have done, and agree for their part what shall stand.

9. As any one company hath despatched any one book in this manner, they shall send it to the rest, to be considered of seriously and judiciously; for his majesty is very careful on this point.

10. If any one company, upon the review of the book so sent, shall doubt or differ upon any places, to send them word thereof, note the places, and therewithal to send their reasons; to which, if they consent not, the difference to be compounded at the general meeting, which is to be of the chief persons of each company, at the end of the work.

11. When any place of special obscurity is doubted of, letters to be directed by authority, to send to any learned in the land, for his judgment in such a place.

12. Letters to be sent from every bishop to the rest of his clergy, admonishing them of this translation in hand; and to move and charge as many as being skilful in the tongues, have taken pains in that kind, to send their particular observations to the company, either at Westminster, Cambridge, or Oxford.

13. The directors in each company to be, the deans of Westminster and Chester,[1] for that place; and the king's professors in Hebrew and Greek in each university.

14. These translations to be used, when they agree better with the text than the bishops' bible itself, viz. Tindal's, Matthew's, Coverdale's, Whitchurch's,[2] Geneva.

[David Norton, *A Textual History of the King James Bible* (Cambridge, UK: Cambridge University Press, 2005), pp. 7–8.]

ENDNOTES:

1. That is, these two deans were responsible for the companies at Westminster.

2. More commonly known as the Great Bible. Whitchurch was the printer of the Great Bible and husband of the widow of Cranmer.

The Jerusalem Chamber, Westminster Abbey, in which the final editing of the AV was done.

APPENDIX 2:

THE 'PRESENTATION' OF THE BIBLE

Early printed books resembled the manuscript book in appearance, there being at first no reason to change what was generally familiar and acceptable. Just like the codex manuscripts described in chapter one, they were simply gatherings of parchment or paper sewn and bound between covers. Printed editions were rarely more than one thousand copies; the average was about two hundred. Gutenberg designed a typeface that looked as similar as possible to the handwritten style of the scribes and copyists, the grandfather of the 'black letter' typeface, popularly called 'gothic'. He also retained the 42-line, two-column format of medieval manuscripts. Fairly soon, however, printers developed a lettering that was lighter and they began to use it on well-spaced, well-arranged pages. The effect of this on Bible presentation, as the possibilities of the new technology were slowly realised, is illustrated here.

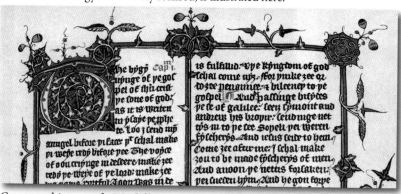

Compare this page of a **Wycliffe manuscript Bible** (*above*) with the pages from the **Gutenberg printed Bible** (*below*) and you will see the imitative nature of the

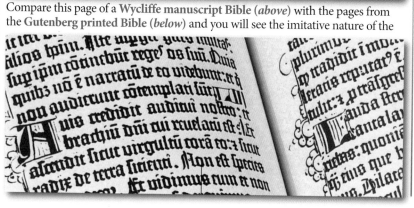

early printed page. It is by no means easy to read.

Next is a detail from a *Coverdale edition (below),* which begins to look a little more familiar. There are page headings, chapter and folio numbers, but no verse

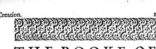

numbers. There are actually chapter contents also, but all at the beginning of each book. It is still black-letter typeface.

Now see a detail from a page of the Geneva Bible (below).

Here is a 'proper' Bible! 'roman' typeface, page headings, chapter contents, verse numbers, marginal notes to help in difficult places: all in a practical size. It is a Bible presented not for liturgical reading but for personal study, the ease of reference inviting shared study. This, in general, is the appearance of the Bible page ever since. (There were printings of some few 'black letter' editions of the Geneva; such are the foibles of men that these now command a significantly greater price on the second-hand book market. The *Douay-Rheims Bible (right), 1582/1610,* was in roman type, but the Authorised Version started in black letter.)

And here is a page from a 1611 Authorised Version (below)

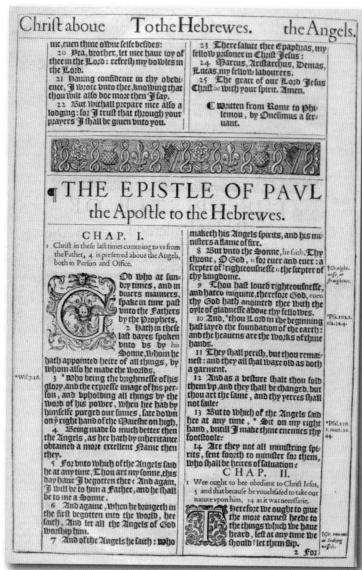

The first page of Hebrews shows the original typeface. There are marginal notes referring to variant translations and cross references to other Bible passages. The chapter is headed by a summary of the contents. There are decorative initial letters for each chapter, and a decorated headpiece to each Biblical book, but no illustrations in the text.

Taken from Quarterly Record *no. 575, April to June 2006, pp. 20–22.*

APPENDIX 3:

WHY THE DIVERSION OF RESOURCES?

Here is an aspect of Bible production, brought challengingly to light in a publication which would not be pro-AV, but yet bewails the swallowing of resources in endless production of more English-language Bibles.

…The English-speaking world has a very large number of different English versions of the Bible, simply because the number of English speakers (many of them with plenty of money to buy multiple copies of the Bible) ensures large financial profits for the publishers. At the same time many people in the world have no Bible in their own language because there is no financial profit to be made by translating and producing one. Much could be achieved if the money currently being spent on developing yet more English language Bibles were dedicated instead to translation in languages with greater need. However, the church also continues to be af-fected by sin, and the injustice will no doubt continue, with more English Bibles being produced while many groups of Christians will continue to be without the word of God in their own language.[1]

This is a sentiment with which the Society heartily agrees. Of the nearly seven thousand living languages, fewer than five hundred are known to have a Bible. Rather than waste our resources upon producing more and more modern English versions, instead we seek, as the Lord leads and enables, to oversee translation projects in other languages, where there are no accurate and therefore trustworthy and reliable Scriptures readily available.

ENDNOTES

1. John DeJong, 'A "Sin Offering" Crouching At the Door? Translation Lessons from an Exegetical Fossil in the Judson Bible', *The Bible Translator*, vol. 61, no. 2, April 2010, p. 92.

APPENDIX 4:

THE COMMITTEE MEN

FIRST WESTMINSTER COMPANY

Responsible for the translation of
Genesis to 2 Kings:

LANCELOT ANDREWES
JOHN OVERALL
ADRIAN SARAVIA
(HADRIAN À SARAVIA)
RICHARD CLARKE
JOHN LAYFIELD
ROBERT TEIGH (TIGHE)
FRANCIS BURLEIGH
GEOFFREY KING
RICHARD THOMSON
WILLIAM BEDWELL

FIRST CAMBRIDGE COMPANY

Responsible for the translation of
*1 Chronicles to
the Song of Solomon:*

EDWARD LIVELEY
JOHN RICHARDSON
LAURENCE CHADERTON
FRANCIS DILLINGHAM
ROGER ANDREWES
THOMAS HARRISON

ROBERT SPALDING
ANDREW BYNG (BING)

FIRST OXFORD COMPANY

Responsible for the translation of
Isaiah to Malachi:

JOHN HARDING
JOHN REYNOLDS (RAINOLDS)
THOMAS HOLLAND
RICHARD KILBY
MILES SMITH
RICHARD BRETT
RICHARD FAIRCLOWE
(DANIEL FEATLEY)

SECOND OXFORD COMPANY

Responsible for the translation of
*the Gospels, Acts of the Apostles,
and the Book of Revelation:*

THOMAS RAVIS
GEORGE ABBOT
RICHARD EEDES
GILES THOMPSON (TOMSON)
SIR HENRY SAVILE
JOHN PERIN (PERYN)
RALPH RAVENS
JOHN HARMAR

SECOND WESTMINSTER COMPANY

responsible for the translation of the
Epistles:

WILLIAM BARLOW
JOHN SPENSER
ROGER FENTON
RALPH HUCHINSON
WILLIAM DAKINS
MICHAEL RABBETT
THOMAS SANDERSON

SECOND CAMBRIDGE COMPANY

responsible for the translation of
the Apocrypha:

JOHN DUPORT
WILLIAM BRANTHWAITE
JEREMIAH RADCLIFFE

SAMUEL WARD
ANDREW DOWNES
JOHN BOYS (BOIS)
T. WARD

JOHN AGLIONBY
LEONARD HUTTEN
THOMAS BILSON
and
RICHARD BANCROFT
are also thought to have participated